NEW YORK NOTARY PUBLIC

PREP BOOK WITH

3 FULL PRACTICE TESTS

THE PINNACLE REVIEW

TABLE OF CONTENTS

INTRODUCTION

Congratulations on your first step to become a notary public in New York State. In this book, you will find all the necessary resources needed to pass the New York notary public exam. The content of this book was developed by professionals that possess extensive knowledge in notary public laws. By analyzing past-administered exams, they identified the items that predict success on the exam and assembled the outlines of laws that govern those questions. These rules of law determine the answers to the questions tested on the exam. We'll take you through all the laws, statutes, and legal terms. Please note that they are unofficial and paraphrased in simple English so that they are easier to read. We'll also give you the opportunity to test your knowledge with true or false questions after every law.

This book is meant to complement the official NYS Division of Licensing Services booklet, Notary Public Licensing Law. Please read the official publication together with this book so that you can conquer the NY notary public exam.

The New York notary public license law booklet can be found on the official New York State Department of State website:
www.dos.ny.gov/licensing/lawbooks/notary.pdf

After you have studied all the content of this book multiple times, you are ready to take on the 3 practice tests. Each practice test contains 40 multiple-choice questions. Set aside 1 hour for each practice test.

Note

Where gender pronouns appear in this booklet, they are meant to refer to both male and female persons.

BECOME A NOTARY PUBLIC IN NEW YORK

Every New York notary public applicant must meet the following requirements.

You must:
- Be at least 18 years old
- Be a person of good moral character
- Reside within the state or maintain a business office in New York
- Have the equivalent of a "common school education"
- Be a U.S. citizen or legal permanent resident
- Complete the application process
- Not be convicted of a crime unless the Secretary of State finds that the crime committed doesn't bar you from commission

As long as all the requirements are met, you are eligible to take the 1-hour New York State notary exam. There are 40 multiple-choice questions on the exam and the applicant must correctly answer at least 70% of the questions to pass. Exam results will be mailed as a "pass slip" once the results are available; typically, within 4-6 weeks. Complete the state application and include the $60 application fee and the original pass slip. The state application can be found on the Division of Licensing Services section of New York State Department of State website:
www.dos.ny.gov/licensing/

NEW YORK NOTARY LAWS

SECTIONS

New York notary laws are broken down into the following sections:

Appointment and Qualifications		
Law	**Section**	**Subject**
Executive Law	130	Appointment of Notaries Public
Executive Law	131	Procedure of Appointment; Fees
Executive Law	132	Certificates of Official Character
Executive Law	133	Certification of Notarial Signatures
Executive Law	140	Commissioner of Deeds, NYC
Election Law	3-200	Commissioner of Elections
	3-400	
Public Officers Law	3	Qualifications for Holding Office
County Law	534	County Clerk; Appointment of Notaries
NYS Constitution	Art. II	Member of Legislature
	Sec. 7	
NYS Constitution	Art. XII Sheriffs	
	Sec. 13a	
Miscellaneous		Disqualifications
Powers and Duties		
Executive Law	134	Signature and Seal of County Clerk
Executive Law	135	Powers and Duties
Executive Law	135a	Acting Without Appointment, Fraud in Office

Executive Law	136	Notarial Fees
Executive Law	137	Statement as to authority
Executive Law	138	Powers of Notaries - Corporations
Executive Law	142-a	Validity of facts
Real Property Law	290	Definitions
Real Property Law	298	Acknowledgments and Proofs within the State
Real Property Law	302	Acknowledgments and Proofs By Married Women
Real Property Law	303	Requisites of Acknowledgments
Real Property Law	304	Proof by Subscribing Witness
Real Property Law	306	Certificate of Acknowledgment or Proof
Real Property Law	309	Acknowledgment by Corporation
Real Property Law	330	Officers Guilty of Malfeasance
Real Property Law	333	When Conveyances Not to Be Recorded
Banking Law	335	Unpaid Rental of Safe Deposit Box
Civil Practice Law and Rules	3113	Taking of Deposition by Notary
Domestic Relation	S11	No Authority to Solemnize Marriage
Public Officers	10	Administering Oath of Public Officer
Restrictions and Violations		
Judiciary Law	484	None but Attorneys to Practice
Judiciary Law	485	Misdemeanor Violations
Judiciary Law	750	Powers of Courts to Punish
Public Officers Law	15	Notary Must Not Act Before Taking/Filing Oath
Public Officers Law	67	Fees of Public Officers
Public Officers Law	69	Fees Prohibited for Administering Certain Oaths

Executive Law	135A	Removal From Office for Misconduct
Penal Law	70.00	Sentence of Imprisonment for Felony
Penal Law	70.15	Sentences of Imprisonment for Misdemeanors
Penal Law	170.10	Forgery in the Second Degree
Penal Law	175.40	Issuing a False Certificate
Penal Law	195.00	Official Misconduct

APPOINTMENT AND QUALIFICATIONS

EXECUTIVE LAW

Section 130 - Appointment of Notaries Public

1. The Secretary of State may appoint and commission as many notaries public for the State of New York as in his or her judgment may be deemed best, whose jurisdiction shall be co-extensive with the boundaries of the state.

The appointment of a notary public shall be for a term of 4 years.

An application for an appointment as notary public shall be in form and set forth such matters as the Secretary of State shall prescribe. Every person appointed as notary public must, at the time of his or her appointment, be a citizen of the United States and either a resident of the State of New York or have an office or place of business in New York State.

A notary public who is a resident of the State and who moves out of the state but still maintains a place of business or an office in New York State does not vacate his or her office as a notary public.

A notary public who is a nonresident and who ceases to have an office or place of business in this state, vacates his or her office as a notary public.

A notary public who is a resident of New York State and moves out of the state and who does not retain an office or place of business in this State shall vacate his or her office as a notary public.

A non-resident who accepts the office of notary public in this State thereby appoints the Secretary of State as the person upon whom process can be served on his or her behalf.

Before issuing to any applicant a commission as notary public, unless he or she be an attorney and counselor at law duly admitted to practice in this state or a court clerk of the Unified Court System who has been appointed to such position after taking a Civil Service promotional examination in the court clerk series of titles, the Secretary of State shall satisfy himself or herself that the applicant is of good moral character, has the equivalent of a common school education and is familiar with the duties and responsibilities of a notary public; provided, however, that where a notary public applies, before the expiration of his or her term, for reappointment with the county clerk or where a person whose term as notary public shall have expired applies within 6 months thereafter for reappointment as a notary public with the county clerk, such qualifying requirements may be waived by the Secretary of State, and further, where an application for reappointment is filed with the county clerk after the expiration of the aforementioned renewal period by a person who failed or was unable to re-apply by reason of his or her induction or enlistment in the armed forces of the United States, such qualifying requirements may also be waived by the Secretary of State, provided such application for reappointment is made within a period of 1 year after the military discharge of the applicant under conditions other than dishonorable.

In any case, the appointment or reappointment of any applicant is in the discretion of the Secretary of State. The Secretary of State may suspend or remove from office, for misconduct, any notary public appointed by him or her but no such removal shall be made unless the person who is sought to be removed shall have been served with a copy of the charges against him or her and have an opportunity of being heard. No person shall be appointed as a notary public under this article who has been convicted, in this State or any other state or territory, of a crime, unless the secretary makes a finding in conformance with all applicable statutory requirements, including those contained in article twenty-three-A of the correction law, that such convictions do not constitute a bar to appointment.

2. A person regularly admitted to practice as an attorney and counselor in the courts of record of this state, whose office for the practice of law is within the State, may be appointed a notary public and retain his office as such notary public although he resides in or removes to an adjoining state. For the purpose of this and the following sections of this article such person shall be deemed a resident of the county where he maintains such office.

SUMMARY

1. The Secretary of State may appoint notaries public for New York State (NYS), whose jurisdiction is the entire state, for a term of 4 years.

At the time of appointment, a person must be a citizen of NYS, and reside or do business within NYS.

A notary public who no longer lives or does business within NYS vacates their position as a notary public.

The Secretary of State is appointed to be served process for any nonresident notaries.

The Secretary of State will ensure notary applicants are of good moral character, has an equivalent of a common school education, and is familiar with duties of a notary, unless the applicant is an attorney or a court clerk in NYS.

These qualifying requirements are waived for reappointments within 6 months of expiration of current notary appointment, or for the exception of enlistment in the armed forces.

The Secretary of State may suspend or remove, for misconduct, any notary public, so long that that notary be served with a copy of the charges against him and have an opportunity to be heard.

No person shall be appointed a notary public who have been convicted in any state of a crime, unless those convictions do no constitute exclusion from appointment such as in New York correction law article 23-A.

2. An attorney who resides in another state but has an office in NYS may be appointed a notary public and retain his office.

For this purpose, an attorney is deemed a resident of the county where he maintains his office.

TRUE OR FALSE?

1. A notary public who does not practice law may retain their appointment upon moving out of state if they intend to return.

✓ Answer key on Page 91

Section 131 - Procedure of appointment; fees and commissions

1. Applicants for a notary public commission shall submit to the Secretary of State with their application the oath of office, duly executed before any person authorized to administer an oath, together with their signature.

2. Upon being satisfied of the competency and good character of applicants for appointment as notaries public, the Secretary of State shall issue a commission to such persons; and the official signature of the applicants and the oath of office filed with such applications shall take effect.

3. The Secretary of State shall receive a non-refundable application fee of $60 from applicants for appointment, which fee shall be submitted together with the application. No further fee shall be paid for the issuance of the commission.

4. A notary public identification card indicating the appointee's name, address, county and

commission term shall be transmitted to the appointee.

5. The commission, duly dated, and a certified copy or the original of the oath of office and the official signature, and $20 apportioned from the application fee shall be transmitted by the Secretary of State to the county clerk in which the appointee resides by the 10th day of the following month.

6. The county clerk shall make a proper index of commissions and official signatures transmitted to that office by the Secretary of State pursuant to the provisions of this section.

7. Applicants for reappointment of a notary public commission shall submit to the county clerk with their application the oath of office, duly executed before any person authorized to administer an oath, together with their signature.

8. Upon being satisfied of the completeness of the application for reappointment, the county clerk shall issue a commission to such persons; and the official signature of the applicants and the oath of office filed with such applications shall take effect.

9. The county clerk shall receive a non-refundable application fee of $60 from each applicant for reappointment, which fee shall be submitted together with the application. No further fee shall be paid for the issuance of the commission.

10. The commission, duly dated, and a certified or original copy of the application, and $40 apportioned from the application fee plus interest as may be required by statute shall be transmitted by the county clerk to the Secretary of State by the 10th day of the following month.

11. The Secretary of State shall make a proper record of commissions transmitted to that office by the county clerk pursuant to the provisions of this section.

12. Except for changes made in an application for reappointment, the Secretary of State shall receive a non-refundable fee of $10 for changing the name or address of a notary public.

13. The Secretary of State may issue a duplicate identification card to a notary public for one lost, destroyed or damaged upon application therefor on a form prescribed by the Secretary of State and upon payment of a nonrefundable fee of $10. Each such duplicate identification card shall have the word "duplicate" stamped across the face thereof, and shall bear the same number as the one it replaces.

SUMMARY

1. Applicants for a notary public must submit their oath of office, performed before any person authorized to administer an oath, along with their signature.

2. Once satisfied of the competence and good character of an applicant, the Secretary of State shall issue a commission, and the official signature of the applicant and the oath of office will take effect.

3. Applicants must pay $60 to the Secretary of State for appointment, no other fee shall be paid.

4. An appointee will receive a notary public identification card with their name, address, county, and commission term.

5. The commission and a certified copy of the oath will be sent to the county clerk where the appointee resides, as well as $20 from the paid fee by the 10th day of the following month.

6. The county clerk shall keep record of commission and official signatures sent by the Secretary of State.

7. Applicants for reappointment will submit to the county clerk their oath, executed before any person authorized, and their signature.

8. Once the application is complete, the county clerk shall issue a commission to the appointee, and their oath and signature shall take effect.

9. The county clerk will receive $60 from each applicant for reappointment. No other fee will be paid.

10. The commission and a certified copy of the oath will be sent to the Secretary of State where the appointee resides, as well as $40 from the paid fee by the 10th day of the following month.

11. The Secretary of State shall keep record of commissions sent by county clerks.

12. The Secretary of State shall receive a $10 fee for changing the name or address of a notary.

13. The Secretary of State may issue a duplicate identification card due to loss or damage for a fee of $10. Each duplicate identification card shall have the word "duplicate" stamped across it.

TRUE OR FALSE?

2. A notary public is allowed one replace ID card free of charge.

✓ Answer key on Page 91

Section 132 - Certificates of official character of notaries public

The Secretary of State or the county clerk of the county in which the commission of a notary public is filed may certify to the official character of such notary public and any notary public may file his autograph signature and a certificate of official character in the office of any county clerk of any county in the State and in any register's office in any county having a register and thereafter such county clerk may certify as to the official character of such notary public.

The Secretary of State shall collect for each certificate of official character issued by him the sum of one dollar. The county clerk and register of any county with whom a certificate of official character has been filed shall collect for filing the same the sum of one dollar. For each certificate of official character issued, with seal attached, by any county clerk, the sum of one dollar shall be collected by him.

SUMMARY

The Secretary of State or the country clerk of the county where the notary public is commissioned, may certify the official character of a notary public. Any notary public may file his signature and certificate of official character in the office of any country clerk or registrar in NYS.

The Secretary of State will collect $1 for each certificate issued by him.

The county clerk and registrar shall collect $1 for filing the certificate, or for issuing one.

TRUE OR FALSE?

3. A notary public can file his signature and certificate of character in any county of the State he is commissioned in.

✓ Answer key on Page 91

Section 133 - Certification of notarial signatures

The county clerk of a county in whose office any notary public has qualified or has filed his autograph signature and a certificate of his official character, shall, when so requested and upon payment of a fee of $3 affix to any certificate of proof or acknowledgment or oath signed by such notary anywhere in the State of New York, a certificate under his hand and seal, stating that a commission or a certificate of his official character with his autograph signature has been filed in his office, and that he was at the time of taking such proof or acknowledgment or oath duly authorized to take the same; that he is well acquainted with the handwriting of such notary public or has compared the signature on the certificate of proof or acknowledgment or oath with the autograph signature deposited in his office by such notary public and believes that the signature is genuine.

An instrument with such certificate of authentication of the county clerk affixed thereto shall be entitled to be read in evidence or to be recorded in any of the counties of this State in respect to which a certificate of a county clerk may be necessary for either purpose.

SUMMARY

A county clerk whose office a notary public has filed his signature or has qualified, shall when requested and upon payment of $3, affix to any certificate, acknowledgment, or oath signed by the notary public in NYS, certify that the notaries public commission or certificate of character has been filed in his office, and that he was authorized to take such proof, acknowledgment or oath; that he is well acquainted with the handwriting of the notary public or has compared his signature to that on file and believes in genuine.

An instrument with such certificate of authentication by the county clerk shall be read in evidence or be recorded in any county of NYS of which a certificate of a county clerk in required.

TRUE OR FALSE?

4. The county clerk can verify that a certificate of a notary has been filed and matches a signed document.

✓ Answer key on Page 91

Section 140 - Executive Law

14. No person who has been removed from office as a commissioner of deeds for the City of New York, as hereinbefore provided, shall thereafter be eligible again to be appointed as such commissioner nor, shall he be eligible thereafter to appoint to the office of notary public.

15. Any person who has been removed from office as aforesaid, who shall, after knowledge of such removal, sign or execute any instrument as a commissioner of deeds or notary public shall be deemed guilty of a misdemeanor.

SUMMARY

14. Someone who was removed from office as a commissioner of deeds for the City of New York is no longer eligible to be appointed again as commission or as a notary.

15. Someone who was removed from office as a commissioner of deeds who, after knowing of their removal, performs an act as the commissioner or as a notary public, will be guilty of a misdemeanor.

TRUE OR FALSE?

5. A person removed from office as a commissioner of deeds can be appointed a notary public following their probation.

✓ Answer key on Page 91

Section 3-200 and 3-400 - Election Law

A commissioner of elections or inspector of elections is eligible for the office of notary public.

SUMMARY

A Commissioner or inspector of elections is eligible to become a notary public.

TRUE OR FALSE?

6. An inspector of elections is eligible to become a notary public.

✓ Answer key on Page 91

Section 3 - Public Officers Law

No person is eligible for the office of notary public who has been convicted of a violation of the selective draft act of the U.S. enacted May 18, 1917, or the acts amendatory or supplemental thereto, or of the federal selective training and service act of 1940 or the acts amendatory thereof or supplemental thereto.

SUMMARY

Any person who has been convicted of a violation of the selective service draft act, the amendments to it, or the federal selective training and service act and its amendments is not eligible to be a notary public.

TRUE OR FALSE?

7. Violating the selective draft act automatically disqualifies a person from being a notary public.

✓ Answer key on Page 91

Section 534 - County Law

Each county clerk shall designate from among the members of his or her staff at least one notary public to be available to notarize documents for the public in each county clerk's office during normal business hours free of charge. Each individual appointed by the county clerk to be a notary public pursuant to this section shall be exempt from the examination fee and application fee required by Section 131 of the Executive Law.

SUMMARY

Each county clerk will have at least one notary public staff member available to notarize documents for the public during normal business hours free of charge.

Each staff member appointed to be a notary public is exempt from the examination fee and application fee.

TRUE OR FALSE?

8. There are no exemptions on who has to pay the fee to become a notary public.

✓ Answer key on Page 91

Notary public - disqualifications

Though a person may be eligible to hold the office of notary the person may be disqualified to act in certain cases by reason of having an interest in the case. To state the rule broadly: if the notary is a party to or directly and pecuniarily interested in the transaction, the person is not capable of acting in that case.

For example, a notary who is a grantee or mortgagee in a conveyance or mortgage is disqualified to take the acknowledgment of the grantor or mortgagor; likewise, a notary who is a trustee in a deed of trust; and, of course, a notary who is the grantor could not take his own acknowledgment.

A notary beneficially interested in the conveyance by way of being secured thereby is not competent to take the acknowledgment of the instrument. In New York the courts have held an acknowledgment taken by a person financially or beneficially interested in a party to conveyance or instrument of which it is a part to be a nullity; and that the acknowledgment of an assignment of a mortgage before one of the assignees is a nullity; and that an acknowledgment by one of the incorporators of the other incorporators who signed a certificate was of no legal effect.

SUMMARY

A notary public may be ineligible to act in certain cases.

If a notary public is a party to, or has a direct interest in the transaction, they are not able to act in that case.

For example, a notary who is the grantor, could not take his own acknowledgment.

If a notary is financially benefited or otherwise benefited from the conveyance, then the acknowledgment is nullified.

POWERS AND DUTIES

EXECUTIVE LAW

Section 134 - Signature and seal of county clerk

The signature and seal of a county clerk, upon a certificate of official character of a notary public or the signature of a county clerk upon a certificate of authentication of the signature and acts of a notary public or commissioner of deeds, may be a facsimile, printed, stamped, photographed or engraved thereon.

SUMMARY

The signature and seal of a county clerk, upon an official character certificate or a certificate of authentication of a notary public, may be facsimile, printed, stamped, photographed, or engraved.

TRUE OR FALSE?

9. The seal of a county clerk on an official character certificate of a notary public must be stamped.

✓ Answer key on Page 91

Section 135 - Powers and duties; in general; of notaries public who are attorneys at law

Every notary public duly qualified is hereby authorized and empowered within and throughout the State to administer oaths and affirmations, to take affidavits and depositions, to receive and certify acknowledgments or proof of deeds, mortgages and powers of attorney and other instruments in writing; to demand acceptance or payment of foreign and inland bills of exchange, promissory notes and obligations in writing, and to protest the same for non-acceptance or non-payment, as the case may require, and, for use in another jurisdiction, to exercise such other powers and duties as by the laws of nations and according to commercial usage, or by the laws of any other government or country may be exercised and performed by notaries public, provided that when exercising such powers he shall set forth the name of such other jurisdiction.

A notary public who is an attorney at law regularly admitted to practice in this State may, in his discretion, administer an oath or affirmation to or take the affidavit or acknowledgment of his client in respect of any matter, claim, action or proceeding.

For any misconduct by a notary public in the performance of any of his powers such notary public shall be liable to the parties injured for all damages sustained by them.

A notary public shall not, directly or indirectly, demand or receive for the protest for the non-payment of any note, or for the non-acceptance or non-payment of any bill of exchange, check or draft and giving the requisite notices and certificates of such protest, including his notarial seal, if affixed thereto, any greater fee or reward than 75 cents for such protest, and 10 cents for each notice, not exceeding five, on any bill or note.

Every notary public having a seal shall, except as otherwise provided, and when requested, affix his seal to such protest free of expense.

SUMMARY

Every notary public is authorized and empowered within NYS to administer oaths and affirmations, take affidavits and depositions, receive or certify acknowledgments or proof of deeds, mortgages and power or attorney and other instruments in writings, and to protest the same for non-acceptance or non-payment as needed.

In other jurisdictions, to exercise such powers and duties by their laws and commercial usage, or by the laws of other governments provided that when using such powers, they name the jurisdiction.

A notary public who is a practicing attorney in NYS may administer an oath or take and affidavit of his client with respect to any matter, claim, action, or proceeding.

Any misconduct by a notary public in the performance of his powers shall make him liable to the parties injured for all damages they sustained.

A notary public shall not charge more than 75 cents for each protest of non-payment, and 10 cents for each notice (limited to 5), and when requested will affix his seal to such protest free of expense.

TRUE OR FALSE?

10.   A notary public is authorized to take affidavits and depositions in the State of New York.

✓ Answer key on Page 91

Section 135-a - Notary public or commissioner of deeds; acting without appointment; fraud in office

1. Any person who holds himself out to the public as being entitled to act as a notary public or commissioner of deeds, or who assumes, uses or advertises the title of notary public or commissioner of deeds, or equivalent terms in any language, in such a manner as to convey the impression that he is a notary public or commissioner of deeds without having first been appointed as notary public or commissioner of deeds, or

2. A notary public or commissioner of deeds, who in the exercise of the powers, or in the performance of the duties of such office shall practice any fraud or deceit, the punishment for which is not otherwise provided for by this act, shall be guilty of a misdemeanor

SUMMARY

1. Any person who advertises to the public that he is a notary public or acts as a notary public without having been appointed a notary, or

2. Any notary who while using his powers practices fraud or deceit, will be guilty of a misdemeanor.

TRUE OR FALSE?

11.   A notary public committing fraud has committed a felony.

✓ Answer key on Page 91

Section 135-b - Advertising by notaries public

1. The provisions of this section shall not apply to attorneys-at-law, admitted to practice in the state of New York.

2. A notary public who advertises his or her services as a notary public in a language other than English shall post with such advertisement a notice in such other language the following statement: "I am not an attorney licensed to practice law and may not give legal

advice about immigration or any other legal matter or accept fees for legal advice."

3. A notary public shall not use terms in a foreign language in any advertisement for his or her services as a notary public that mean or imply that the notary public is an attorney licensed to practice in the state of New York or in any jurisdiction of the United States. The secretary shall designate by rule or regulation the terms in a foreign language that shall be deemed to mean or imply that a notary public is licensed to practice law in the state of New York and the use of which shall be prohibited by notary publics who are subject to this section.

4. For purposes of this section, "advertisement" shall mean and include material designed to give notice of or to promote or describe the services offered by a notary public for profit and shall include business cards, brochures, and notices, whether in print or electronic form.

5. Any person who violates any provision of this section or any rule or regulation promulgated by the secretary may be liable for civil penalty of up to one thousand dollars. The secretary of state may suspend a notary public upon a second violation of any of the provisions of this section and may remove from office a notary public upon a third violation of any of the provisions of this section, provided that the notary public shall have been served with a copy of the charges against him or her and been given an opportunity to be heard. The civil penalty provided for by this subdivision shall be recoverable in an action instituted by the attorney general on his or her own initiative or at the request of the secretary.

6. The secretary may promulgate rules and regulations governing the provisions of this section, including the size and type of statements that a notary public is required by this section to post.

SUMMARY

1. This section does not apply to attorneys practicing in NYS.

2. A notary public who advertises in a language other than English must include the following:

"I am not an attorney licensed to practice law and may not give legal advice about immigration or any other legal matter or accept fees for legal advice."

3. A notary may not use words in a foreign language that imply he is a licensed attorney. The secretary shall designate which foreign terms imply that a notary public is licensed as

previously mentioned, and the use shall be prohibited.

4. "Advertisement" means material designed to give notice of or to promote ones services as a notary public for profit, and shall include business cards, brochures, and notices in print or electronic form.

5. Anyone violating one of these rules may be liable for a civil penalty up to $1,000.

The Secretary of State may suspend a notary public for a second violation of these rules, and may remove a notary public upon a third violation, provided the notary public has the opportunity to be heard.

The civil penalty shall be recoverable by the attorney general's initiative, or at request of the secretary.

6. The secretary may announce rules and regulations governing this section, including the size and type of statements that a notary public is required by this section to post.

TRUE OR FALSE?

12.   A notary public who is also an attorney may not advertise legal services in a foreign language.

✓ Answer key on Page 91

Section 136 - Notarial fees

A notary public shall be entitled to the following fees:

1. For administering an oath or affirmation, and certifying the same when required, except where another fee is specifically prescribed by statute, $2.

2. For taking and certifying the acknowledgment or proof of execution of a written instrument, by one person, $2, and by each additional person, $2, for swearing such witness thereto, $2.

SUMMARY

A notary public is entitled to the following fees:

2. For administering an oath or affirmation, and certifying the same, except when another fee is prescribed by statute, $2.

3. For taking and certifying the acknowledgment or proof of execution of a written instrument, for one person, $2, and for each additional person, $2, and for swearing a witness, $2.

TRUE OR FALSE?

13.   A notary public may charge $2 for administering an oath.

✓ Answer key on Page 91

Section 137 - Statement as to authority of notaries public

In exercising his powers pursuant to this article, a notary public, in addition to the venue of his act and his signature, shall print, typewrite, or stamp beneath his signature in black ink, his name, the words "Notary Public State of New York," the name of the county in which he originally qualified, and the date upon which his commission expires and, in addition, wherever required, a notary public shall also include the name of any county in which his certificate of official character is filed, using the words "Certificate filed .... County."

A notary public who is duly licensed as an attorney and counselor at law in this State may in his discretion, substitute the words "Attorney and Counselor at Law" for the words "Notary Public."

A notary public who has qualified or who has filed a certificate of official character in the office of the clerk in a county or counties within the City of New York must also affix to each instrument his official number or numbers in black ink, as given to him by the clerk or clerks of such county or counties at the time such notary qualified in such county or counties and, if the instrument is to be recorded in an office of the register of the City of New York in any county within such city and the notary has been given a number or numbers by such register or his predecessors in any county or counties, when his autographed signature and certificate are filed in such office or offices pursuant to this chapter, he shall also affix such number or numbers. No official act of such notary public shall be held invalid on account of the failure to comply with these provisions. If any notary public shall wilfully fail to comply with any of the provisions of this section, he shall be subject to disciplinary action by the secretary of state.

In all the courts within this State the certificate of a notary public, over his signature, shall be received as presumptive evidence of the facts contained in such certificate; provided, that any person interested as a party to a suit may contradict, by other evidence, the certificate of a notary public.

SUMMARY

In performing his duties, a notary public, in addition to the location of his act and signature, shall print, typewrite, or stamp beneath his signature in black ink, his name, the words **"Notary Public State of New York,"** the name of the county which he first qualified, date commission expires, and where required, the name of any county where his certificate of official character is filed using the words **"Certificate filed…County."** This is also called the statement of authority.

An attorney in the state may substitute notary public for the words **"Attorney and Counselor at Law."**

A notary public who has qualified or filed a certificate in a county within New York City must also affix his official number in black ink, given to him by the clerks in the county at the time the notary qualified.

No official act will be deemed invalid for failure to comply with this section.

Any notary public who willfully fails to comply with this section shall be subject to discipline by the Secretary of State.

In all courts in the state, the certificate of a notary public over his signature shall be received as presumptive evidence of the facts within, provided that another party may contradict with other evidence the certificate of a notary public.

TRUE OR FALSE?

14.   "Notary Public State of New York" must be included on every signature, regardless if the notary if also an attorney.

✓ Answer key on Page 91

Section 138 - Powers of notaries public or other officers who are stockholders, directors, officers or employees of a corporation

A notary public, justice of the supreme court, a judge, clerk, deputy clerk, or special deputy clerk of a court, an official examiner of title, or the mayor or recorder of a city, a justice of the peace, surrogate, special surrogate, special county judge, or commissioner of deeds, who is a stockholder, director, officer or employee of a corporation may take the acknowledgment or proof of any party to a written instrument executed to or by such corporation, or administer an oath of any other stockholder, director, officer, employee or agent of such corporation, and such notary public may protest for non- acceptance or non-payment, bills of exchange, drafts, checks, notes and other negotiable instruments owned or held for collection by such corporation; but none of the officers above named shall take the acknowledgment or proof of a written instrument by or to a corporation of which he is a stockholder, director, officer or employee, if such officer taking such acknowledgment or proof to be a party executing such instrument, either individually or as representative of such corporation, nor shall a notary public protest any negotiable instruments owned or held for collection by such corporation, if such notary public be individually a party to such instrument, or have a financial interest in the subject of same.

All such acknowledgments or proofs of deeds, mortgages or other written instruments, relating to real property heretofore taken before any of the officers aforesaid are confirmed. This act shall not affect any action or legal proceeding now pending.

SUMMARY

A notary public, justice of the supreme court, judge, clerk, deputy clerk, special deputy clerk of court, official examiner of title, the mayor or recorder of a city, justice of the peace, surrogate, special surrogate, special county judge, or commissioner of deeds, who is a stockholder, director, officer or employee of a corporation may take the acknowledgment of any party to a written instrument executed by such corporation or administer the oath of any shareholder, director, officer, employee, or agent of such corporation.

A notary public may protest for non-payment, but no officer shall take the acknowledgment of a corporation which he is involved in.

TRUE OR FALSE?

15.   A notary public who is a stockholder of a company may take proof to a written instrument executed to that company.

✓ Answer key on Page 91

Section 142-a - Validity of acts of notaries public and commissioners of

deeds notwithstanding certain defects

1. Except as provided in subdivision three of this section, the official certificates and other acts heretofore or hereafter made or performed of notaries public and commissioners of deeds heretofore or hereafter and prior to the time of their acts appointed or commissioned as such shall not be deemed invalid, impaired or in any manner defective, so far as they may be affected, impaired or questioned by reason of defects described in subdivision two of this section.

2. This section shall apply to the following defects:

    a. ineligibility of the notary public or commissioner of deeds to be appointed or commissioned as such;

    b. misnomer or misspelling of name or other error made in his appointment or commission;

    c. omission of the notary public or commissioner of deeds to take or file his official oath or otherwise qualify;

    d. expiration of his term, commission or appointment;

    e. vacating of his office by change of his residence, by acceptance of another public office, or by other action on his part;

    f. the fact that the action was taken outside the jurisdiction where the notary public or commissioner of deeds was authorized to act.

3. No person shall be entitled to assert the effect of this section to overcome a defect described in subdivision two if he knew of the defect or if the defect was apparent on the face of the certificate of the notary public or commissioner of deeds; provided however, that this subdivision shall not apply after the expiration of six months from the date of the act of the notary public or commissioner of deeds.

4. After the expiration of six months from the date of the official certificate or other act of the commissioner of deeds, subdivision one of this section shall be applicable to a defect consisting in omission of the certificate of a commissioner of deeds to state the date on which and the place in which an act was done, or consisting of an error in such statement.

5. This section does not relieve any notary public or commissioner of deeds from criminal

liability imposed by reason of his act, or enlarge the actual authority of any such officer, nor limit any other statute or rule of law by reason of which the act of a notary public or commissioner of deeds, or the record thereof, is valid or is deemed valid in any case.

SUMMARY

1. Except as provided in subdivision 3, the official certificate and other acts made by notaries and commissioners of deeds shall not be invalid, impaired, or questioned by reason of defects unless they satisfy a requirement of subdivision 2.

2. This section lists applicable defects:

    a. Ineligibility of the notary or commissioner of deeds to be appointed as such;

    b. Misnomer or misspelling of the name or other error made;

    c. Omission of the notary or commissioner to take or file his oath;

    d. Expiration of his term, commission, or appointment;

    e. Vacating the post by moving or accepting a new position;

    f. The action was outside the jurisdiction of the notary public or commissioner.

3. Nobody can claim relief due to defect if they knew of the defect or it was apparent on the certificate; provided that this subdivision shall not apply 6 months after the act.

4. After 6 months from the act, subdivision 1 shall be applicable to a defect of omission of the certificate of a commissioner of deeds to state the date and place the act was done, or consisting of an error in such statement.

5. This does not relieve a notary public or commission from criminal liability based on his act, enlarge authority, or limit any other statute or law that makes his actions valid or invalid.

TRUE OR FALSE?

16.   A person can file a claim for defect if the defect was known about upon when it occurred.

✓ Answer key on Page 91

REAL PROPERTY LAW

Section 290 - Definitions; effect of article

3. The term "conveyance" includes every written instrument, by which any estate or interest in real property is created, transferred, mortgaged or assigned, or by which the title to any real property may be affected, including an instrument in execution of power, although the power be one of revocation only, and an instrument postponing or subordinating a mortgage lien; except a will, a lease for a term not exceeding three years, an executory contract for the sale or purchase of lands, and an instrument containing a power to convey real property as the agent or attorney for the owner of such property.

SUMMARY

3. Conveyance includes every written instrument that any estate or interest in real property is created, transferred, mortgaged, or assigned, or where any title to any real property is affected, including an instrument in execution of power, including revocation, and an instrument postponing or subordinating a mortgage lien.

Exceptions are a will, a lease for less than 3 years, an executory contract for sale or purchase of lands, an instrument containing power to convey property as the agent or attorney.

TRUE OR FALSE?

17. A lease for 2 years is an example of a conveyance.

✓ Answer key on Page 91

Section 298 - Acknowledgments and proofs within the state

The acknowledgment or proof, within this state, of a conveyance of real property situate in this State may be made:

1. At any place within the state, before

   a. a justice of the supreme court;

   b. an official examiner of title;

   c. an official referee; or

d. a notary public.

2. Within the district wherein such officer is authorized to perform official duties, before:

a. a judge or clerk of any court of record;

b. a commissioner of deeds outside of the City of New York, or a commissioner of deeds of the City of New York within the five counties comprising the City of New York

c. the mayor or recorder of a city;

d. a surrogate, special surrogate, or special county judge; or

e. the county clerk or other recording officer of a county.

3. Before a justice of the peace, town councilman, village police justice or a judge of any court of inferior local jurisdiction, anywhere within the county containing the town, village or city in which he is authorized to perform official duties.

SUMMARY

Within NYS, the acknowledgment of proof of a conveyance of real property may be made:

1. At any place within the state, before

a. A justice of the supreme court;

b. An official examiner of title;

c. An official referee; or

d. A notary public.

2. Within the district of the conveyance, it can be performed before the following:

a. A judge or clerk of any court of record;

b. A commissioner of deeds outside the City of NY, or a commissioner of deeds of the City of NY within its counties;

c. The mayor or recorder of a city;

d. A surrogate, special surrogate, or special county judge; or

e. The county clerk or other recording officer of a county.

3. Before a justice of the peace, town councilman, village police justice, or a judge of any lower court, for conveyances within the county containing the town in which they officially work.

TRUE OR FALSE?

18. A notary public may certify the acknowledgment of proof for any conveyance within the state.

✓ Answer key on Page 91

Section 302 - Acknowledgments and proofs by married women

The acknowledgment or proof of a conveyance of real property, within the state, or of any other written instrument, may be made by a married woman the same as if unmarried.

SUMMARY

The acknowledgment of proof of conveyance made by married women, same as if unmarried.

TRUE OR FALSE?

19. Married women have the same rights as unmarried in conveyances.

✓ Answer key on Page 91

Section 303 - Requisites of acknowledgments

An acknowledgment must not be taken by any officer unless he knows or has satisfactory evidence, that the person making it is the person described in and who executed such instrument.

SUMMARY

An acknowledgment must not be taken by anyone unless they know or have evidence the person making it is the person described.

TRUE OR FALSE?

20.   A notary public does not need to verify the identity of the person they are taking an acknowledgment from.

✓ Answer key on Page 91

Section 304 - Proof by subscribing witness

When the execution of a conveyance is proved by a subscribing witness, such witness must state his own place of residence, and if his place of residence is in a city, the street and street number, if any thereof, and that he knew the person described in and who executed the conveyance. The proof must not be taken unless the officer is personally acquainted with such witness, or has satisfactory evidence that he is the same person, who was a subscribing witness to the conveyance.

SUMMARY

When there is a subscribing witness in the execution of a conveyance, the witness must state his full address, and that he knows the person who executed the conveyance.

The officer must know, or have proof that he is the same person who is listed as a subscribing witness.

TRUE OR FALSE?

21.   A subscribing witness must know the person executing the conveyance.

✓ Answer key on Page 91

Section 306 - Certificate of acknowledgment or proof

A person taking the acknowledgment or proof of a conveyance must endorse thereupon or attach thereto, a certificate, signed by himself, stating all the matters required to be done, known, or proved on the taking of such acknowledgment or proof; together with the name and substance of the testimony of each witness examined before him, and if a subscribing witness, his place of residence.

SUMMARY

A person taking the acknowledgment or proof of conveyance must include a signed certificate stating the details of the conveyance with the name and testimony of the witnesses and the addresses for any witnesses who signed.

TRUE OR FALSE?

22.   When taking the acknowledgment or proof of conveyance, a notary public needs to include a certificate with the details of the conveyance, and the name and testimony of the witnesses only.

✓ Answer key on Page 91

Section 309-a - Uniform forms of certificates of acknowledgment or proof within this state

1. The certificate of an acknowledgment, within this State, or a conveyance or other instrument in respect to real property situate in this State, by a person, must conform substantially with the following form, the blanks being properly filled:

State of New York)

) ss.:

County of . . . .)

   On the . . . . . . day of . . . . . . in the year . . . . . . before me, the undersigned, personally appeared . . . . . ., personally known to me or proved to me on the basis of satisfactory evidence to be the individual(s) whose name(s) is (are) subscribed to the within instrument and acknowledged to me that he/she/they executed the same in his/her/their capacity(ies), and that by his/her/their signature(s) on the instrument, the individual(s), or the person upon behalf of which the individual(s) acted, executed the instrument.

   (Signature and office of individual taking acknowledgment.)

2. The certificate for a proof of execution by a subscribing witness, within this state, of a

conveyance or other instrument made by any person in respect to real property situate in this state, must conform substantially with the following form, the blanks being properly filled:

State of New York)
) ss.:
County of . . . .)
    On the . . . . . . day of . . . . . in the year . . . . . before me, the undersigned, personally appeared . . . . . ., the subscribing witness to the foregoing instrument, with whom I am personally acquainted, who, being by me duly sworn, did depose and say that he/she/they reside(s) in . . . . . . (if the place of residence is in a city, include the street and street number, if any, thereof); that he/she/they know(s) . . . . . . to be the individual described in and who executed the foregoing instrument; that said subscribing witness was present and saw said . . . . . . execute the same; and that said witness at the same time subscribed his/her/their name(s) as a witness thereto.
    (Signature and office of individual taking proof).

3. A certificate of an acknowledgment or proof taken under Section 300 of this article shall include the additional information required by that section.

4. For the purposes of this section, the term "person" means any corporation, joint stock company, estate, general partnership (including any registered limited liability partnership or foreign limited liability partnership), limited liability company (including a professional service limited liability company), foreign limited liability company (including a foreign professional service limited liability company), joint venture, limited partnership, natural person, attorney in fact, real estate investment trust, business trust or other trust, custodian, nominee or any other individual or entity in its own or any representative capacity.

SUMMARY

1. The certificate of an acknowledgment in NYS or a conveyance must substantially conform the following form (blank spaces filled appropriately):

State of New York)
) ss.:
County of . . . .)
    On the . . . . . . day of . . . . . . in the year . . . . . . before me, the undersigned, personally appeared . . . . . ., personally known to me or proved to me on the basis of satisfactory evidence to be the individual(s) whose name(s) is (are) subscribed to the within instrument and acknowledged to me that he/she/they executed the same in his/her/their capacity(ies), and that by his/her/their signature(s) on the instrument, the individual(s), or the person upon behalf of which the individual(s) acted, executed the instrument.

(Signature and office of individual taking acknowledgment.)

2. The certificate for proof of execution by a subscribing witness for a conveyance in respect to real property must conform the following form (blank spaces filled appropriately):

State of New York   )
) ss.:
County of . . . .   )

On the . . . . . . day of . . . . . . in the year . . . . . before me, the undersigned, personally appeared . . . . . ., the subscribing witness to the foregoing instrument, with whom I am personally acquainted, who, being by me duly sworn, did depose and say that he/she/they reside(s) in . . . . . . (if the place of residence is in a city, include the street and street number, if any, thereof); that he/she/they know(s) . . . . . . to be the individual described in and who executed the foregoing instrument; that said subscribing witness was present and saw said . . . . . . execute the same; and that said witness at the same time subscribed his/her/their name(s) as a witness thereto.

(Signature and office of individual taking proof).

3. A certificate of acknowledgment taken under section 300 shall include required information.

4. For this section the term "person" means any individual or entity in its own or any representative capacity.

TRUE OR FALSE?

23.   If following the format in 309-a, a notary public does not need to include any other information.

✓ Answer key on Page 91

Section 309-b - Uniform forms of certificates of acknowledgment or proof without this state

1. The certificate of an acknowledgment, without this State, of a conveyance or other instrument with respect to real property situate in this State, by a person, may conform substantially with the following form, the blanks being properly filled:

State, District of Columbia,   )

Territory, Possession, or   ) ss.:
Foreign Country   )

On the . . . . . . day of . . . . . . in the year . . . . . before me, the undersigned, personally appeared . . . . . ., personally known to me or proved to me on the basis of satisfactory evidence to be the individual(s) whose name(s) is (are) subscribed to the within instrument and acknowledged to me that he/she/they executed the same in his/her/their capacity(ies), and that by his/her/their signature(s) on the instrument, the individual(s), or the person upon behalf of which the individual(s) acted, executed the instrument.

(Signature and office of individual taking acknowledgment.)

2. The certificate for a proof of execution by a subscribing witness, without this State, of a conveyance or other instrument made by any person in respect to real property situate in this State, may conform substantially with the following form, the blanks being properly filled:

State, District of Columbia,)
Territory, Possession, or   ) ss.:
Foreign Country   )

On the . . . . . . day of . . . . . . in the year . . . . . . before me, the undersigned, personally appeared . . . . . ., the subscribing witness to the foregoing instrument, with whom I am personally acquainted, who, being by me duly sworn, did depose and say that he/she resides in . . . . . . (if the place of residence is in a city, include the street and street number, if any, thereof); that he/she knows . . . . . . to be the individual described in and who executed the foregoing instrument; that said subscribing witness was present and saw said . . . . . . execute the same; and that said witness at the same time subscribed his/her name as a witness thereto.

(Signature and office of individual taking proof.)

3. No provision of this section shall be construed to:

a. modify the choice of laws afforded by Section 299-a and 301-a of this article pursuant to which an acknowledgment or proof may be taken;

b. modify any requirement of Section 307 of this article;

c. modify any requirement for a seal imposed by subdivision one of Section 308 of this article;

d. modify any requirement concerning a certificate of authentication imposed by Section 308, 311, 312, 314, or 318 of this article; or

e. modify any requirement imposed by any provision of this article when the certificate of acknowledgment or proof purports to be taken in the manner prescribed by the laws of another state, the District of Columbia, territory, possession, or foreign country.

4. A certificate of an acknowledgment or proof taken under Section 300 of this article shall include the additional information required by that section.

5. For the purposes of this section, the term "person" means a person as defined in subdivision 4 of Section 309-a of this article.

6. The inclusion within the body (other than the jurat) of a certificate of acknowledgment or proof made under this section or the city or other political subdivision and the state or country or other place the acknowledgment was taken shall be deemed. A non-substantial variance from the form of a certificate authorized by this section.

SUMMARY

1. The certificate of an acknowledgment, without this state, for a conveyance may substantially conform this form (blank spaces filled appropriately):

State, District of Columbia,)
Territory, Possession, or   ) ss.:
Foreign Country   )
On the . . . . . . day of . . . . . . in the year . . . . . . before me, the undersigned, personally appeared . . . . . ., personally known to me or proved to me on the basis of satisfactory evidence to be the individual(s) whose name(s) is (are) subscribed to the within instrument and acknowledged to me that he/she/they executed the same in his/her/their capacity(ies), and that by his/her/their signature(s) on the instrument, the individual(s), or the person upon behalf of which the individual(s) acted, executed the instrument.
(Signature and office of individual taking acknowledgment.)

2. The certificate for a proof of execution by a subscribing witness, without the state, should conform the following form (blank spaces filled appropriately):

State, District of Columbia,)
Territory, Possession, or   ) ss.:
Foreign Country   )
On the . . . . . . day of . . . . . . in the year . . . . . . before me, the undersigned, personally appeared . . . . . ., the subscribing witness to the foregoing instrument, with whom I am personally acquainted, who, being by me duly sworn, did depose and say that he/she resides in . . . . . . (if the place of residence is in a city, include the street and street number, if any,

thereof); that he/she knows . . . . . . to be the individual described in and who executed the foregoing instrument; that said subscribing witness was present and saw said . . . . . . execute the same; and that said witness at the same time subscribed his/her name as a witness thereto.

(Signature and office of individual taking proof.)

3. No provision of this section should be interpreted to:

    a. Modify the choice of law based on sections 299-a and 301-a of this article;

    b. Modify a requirement of section 307;

    c. Modify seal requirements of section 308;

    d. Modify certificate of authentication requirements of sections 308, 311, 312, 314, or 318;

    e. Modify any requirements of this article when following the law of another jurisdiction.

4. A certificate of an acknowledgment or proof taken under section 300 shall include the additional information required.

5. For this section, a person is defined in subdivision 4 of section 309-a.

6. The inclusion of location within a proof of acknowledgment will be viewed as a non-substantial variance from the previous form.

TRUE OR FALSE?

24. Including the location of the proof of acknowledgment is a substantial error and variation from the template.

✓ Answer key on Page 91

Section 330 - Officers guilty of malfeasance liable for damages

An officer authorized to take the acknowledgment or proof of a conveyance or other instrument, or to certify such proof or acknowledgment, or to record the same, who is guilty of malfeasance or fraudulent practice in the execution of any duty prescribed by law in relation thereto, is liable in damages to the person injured.

SUMMARY

An officer authorized to take and acknowledgment of proof who is guilty of malfeasance or fraud is liable in damages to those injured.

TRUE OR FALSE?

25. A notary public guilty of fraud is liable for damages to the injured party.

✓ Answer key on Page 91

Section 333 - When conveyances of real property not to be recorded

2. A recording officer shall not record or accept for record any conveyance of real property, unless said conveyance in its entirety and the certificate of acknowledgment or proof and the authentication thereof, other than proper names therein which may be in another language provided they are written in English letters or characters, shall be in the English language, or unless such conveyance, certificate of acknowledgment or proof, and the authentication thereof be accompanied by and have attached thereto a translation in the English language duly executed and acknowledged by the person or persons making such conveyance and proved and authenticated, if need be, in the manner required of conveyances for recording in this state, or, unless such conveyance, certificate of acknowledgment or proof, and the authentication thereof be accompanied by and have attached thereto a translation in the English language made by a person duly designated for such purpose by the county judge of the county where it is desired to record such conveyance or a justice of the supreme court and be duly signed, acknowledged and certified under oath or upon affirmation by such person before such judge, to be a true and accurate translation and contain a certification of the designation of such person by such judge.

SUMMARY

2. A recording officer should not accept any conveyance of real property that is in a foreign language, other than names (provided they are written in English), unless a translation is given that is authenticated, or a translation is provided by a person duly appointed by the county judge of the county or justice of the supreme court and certified under oath to be a true and accurate translation.

TRUE OR FALSE?

26.   A recording officer fluent in another language may accept a conveyance in that language.

✓ Answer key on Page 91

SPECIAL NOTE

By reason of changes in certain provisions of the Real Property Law, any and all limitations on the authority of a notary public to act as such in any part of the State have been removed; a notary public may now, in addition to administering oaths or taking affidavits anywhere in the State, take acknowledgments and proofs of conveyances anywhere in the State.

The need for a certificate of authentication of a county clerk as a prerequisite to recording or use in evidence in this State of the instrument acknowledged or proved has been abolished. The certificate of authentication may possibly be required where the instrument is to be recorded or used in evidence outside the jurisdiction of the State.

Effective September 23, 2012, recording officers (County Clerks) may receive and record digitized paper documents and electronic records affecting real property, including real property transfer documents such as deeds, mortgages, notes and accompanying documents. The Office of Information Technology Services (ITS) has promulgated rules and regulations to support the implementation of electronic recording by local recording officers.

Section 335 - Banking Law

If the rental fee of any safe deposit box is not paid, or after the termination of the lease for such box, and at least 30 days after giving proper notice to the lessee, the lessor (bank) may, in the presence of a notary public, open the safe deposit box, remove and inventory the contents. The notary public shall then file with the lessor a certificate under seal which states the date of the opening of the safe deposit box, the name of the lessee, and a list of the contents. Within 10 days of the opening of the safe deposit box, a copy of this certificate must be mailed to the lessee at his last known postal address.

SUMMARY

If the rental fee for a security box is not paid or after termination of said rental and 30 days after giving notice, the bank may, with a notary public present, open the box, and remove and inventory contents.

The notary public shall then file with the bank, under seal, the name of lessee and list of contents which must be mailed to the lessee within 10 days.

TRUE OR FALSE?

27. A letter must be sent to the lessee of a security box within 30 days of the bank opening it.

✓ Answer key on Page 91

Rule 3113 - Civil Practice Law and Rules

This rule authorizes a deposition to be taken before a notary public in a civil proceeding.

SUMMARY

A notary public may take a deposition in a civil proceeding.

TRUE OR FALSE?

28. A notary public may take a deposition is a civil proceeding.

✓ Answer key on Page 91

Section 11 - Domestic Relations Law

A notary public has no authority to solemnize marriages; nor may a notary public take the acknowledgment of parties and witnesses to a written contract of marriage.

SUMMARY

A notary public has no authority to officiate marriages or take the acknowledgment of witnesses to a marriage contract.

TRUE OR FALSE?

29. A notary public may take the acknowledgment for witnesses of a marriage.

✓ Answer key on Page 91

Section 10 - Public Officers Law

Official oaths, permits the oath of a public officer to be administered by a notary public.

SUMMARY

The oath of a public officer can be administered by a notary public.

TRUE OR FALSE?

30.   A notary public can administer the oath of a public officer.

✓ Answer key on Page 91

RESTRICTIONS AND VIOLATIONS

JUDICIARY LAW

Section 484 - None but attorneys to practice in the state

No natural person shall ask or receive, directly or indirectly, compensation for appearing for a person other than himself as attorney in any court or before any magistrate, or for preparing deeds, mortgages, assignments, discharges, leases or any other instruments affecting real estate, wills, codicils, or any other instrument affecting the disposition of property after death, or decedents' estates, or pleadings of any kind in any action brought before any court of record in this state, or make it a business to practice for another as an attorney in any court or before any magistrate unless he has been regularly admitted to practice, as an attorney or counselor, in the courts of record in the state; but nothing in this section shall apply

    1. to officers of societies for the prevention of cruelty, duly appointed, when exercising the special powers conferred upon such corporations under Section 1403 of the Not-for-Profit Corporation Law; or

    2. to law students who have completed at least 2 semesters of law school or persons who have graduated from a law school, who have taken the examination for admittance to practice law in the courts of record in the state immediately available after graduation from law school, or the examination immediately available after being notified by the board of law examiners that they failed to pass said exam, and who have not been notified by the board of law examiners that they have failed to pass two such examinations, acting under the supervision of a legal aid organization, when such students and persons are acting under a program approved by the appellate division of the supreme court of the department in which the principal office of such organization is located and specifying the extent to which such students and persons may engage in activities prohibited by this statute; or

    3. to persons who have graduated from a law school approved pursuant to the rules of the court of appeals for the admission of attorneys and counselors-at-law and who have taken the examination for admission to practice as an attorney and counselor-at-law immediately available after graduation from law school or the examination immediately available after being notified by the board of law examiners that they failed to pass said exam, and who have not been notified by the board of law examiners that they have failed to pass two such examinations, when such persons are acting under the supervision of the state or a subdivision thereof or of any officer or agency of the state or a subdivision thereof, pursuant to a program approved by the appellate division of the supreme court of the

department within which such activities are taking place and specifying the extent to which they may engage in activities otherwise prohibited by this statute and those powers of the supervising governmental entity or officer in connection with which they may engage in such activities.

SUMMARY

No person should receive compensation for appearing for another person as attorney in court, or for preparing real estate transactions, or any matter brought before a court, unless he is an attorney admitted to practice in NYS. This does not apply to:

1. Officers of society for the prevention of cruelty appointed when exercising special powers under section 1403 of the Not-for-Profit Corporation Law, or

2. Law students who have completed 2 semesters or have graduated from law school and took the bar after graduation but failed (only once) and are working under the supervision of a legal aid organization when the program has been approved by the appellate division of the supreme court; or

3. A graduate of law school who took the bar after graduation but failed (only once) and are working under the supervision of the state when it was approved by the appellate division of the supreme court.

TRUE OR FALSE?

31.   A law student may work under the supervision of an appellate court approved legal aid organization after 1 semester of school.

✓ Answer key on Page 91

Section 485 - Violation of certain preceding sections a misdemeanor

Any person violating the provisions of Section 478, 479, 480, 481, 482, 483 or 484, shall be guilty of a misdemeanor.

SUMMARY

Anyone violating the provisions of sections 478, 479, 480, 481, 482, 483 or 484 shall be guilty of a misdemeanor.

TRUE OR FALSE?

32. Violation of section 484 is a felony.

✓ Answer key on Page 91

Section 750 - Power of courts to punish for criminal contempts

The supreme court has power under this section to punish for a criminal contempt any person who unlawfully practices or assumes to practice law; and a proceeding under this subdivision may be instituted on the court's own motion or on the motion of any officer charged with the duty of investigating or prosecuting unlawful practice of law, or by any bar association incorporated under the laws of this State.

SUMMARY

The supreme court has the power to punish for criminal contempt anyone who practices law unlawfully, and a proceeding may be initiated by the court's own motion, or anyone charged to investigate the unlawful practice of law in NYS.

TRUE OR FALSE?

33. The supreme court may punish individuals for unlawful practice of law.

✓ Answer key on Page 91

Illegal practice of law by notary public

To make it a business to practice as an attorney at law, not being a lawyer, is a crime. "Counsel and advice, the drawing of agreements, the organization of corporations and preparing papers connected therewith, the drafting of legal documents of all kinds, including wills, are activities which have been long classed as law practice." (*People v. Alfani*, 227 NY 334, 339.)

SUMMARY

It is a crime to practice law as an attorney and while not being a lawyer.

TRUE OR FALSE?

34.   A notary public who is not a lawyer may draft legal documents for a friend's business.

✓ Answer key on Page 91

Wills

The execution of wills under the supervision of a notary public acting in effect as a lawyer, "cannot be too strongly condemned, not only for the reason that it means an invasion of the legal profession, but for the fact that testators thereby run the risk of frustrating their own solemnly declared intentions and rendering worthless maturely considered plans for the disposition of estates whose creation may have been the fruit of lives of industry and self-denial." (*Matter of Flynn*, 142 Misc. 7.)

PUBLIC OFFICERS LAWS

Notary must not act before taking and filing oath of office. The Public Officers Law (Section 15) provides that a person who executes any of the functions of a public office without having taken and duly filed the required oath of office, as prescribed by law, is guilty of a misdemeanor. A notary public is a public officer.

SUMMARY

A notary public is guilty of a misdemeanor if he performs any duties of a notary before taking and filing oath of office.

TRUE OR FALSE?

35.   A notary public may administer an oath the same day his oath of office has been taken and filed.

✓ Answer key on Page 91

Section 67 - Fees of public officers

1. Each public officer upon whom a duty is expressly imposed by law, must execute the same without fee or reward, except where a fee or other compensation therefor is expressly

allowed by law.

2. An officer or other person, to whom a fee or other compensation is allowed by law, for any service, shall not charge or receive a greater fee or reward, for that service, than is so allowed.

3. An officer, or other person, shall not demand or receive any fee or compensation, allowed to him by law for any service, unless the service was actually rendered by him; except that an officer may demand in advance his fee, where he is, by law, expressly directed or permitted to require payment thereof, before rendering the service.

4. An officer or other person, who violates either of the provisions contained in this section, is liable, in addition to the punishment prescribed by law for the criminal offense, to an action in behalf of the person aggrieved, in which the plaintiff is entitled to treble damages.

A notary public subjects himself to criminal prosecution, civil suit and possible removal by asking or receiving more than the statutory allowance, for administering the ordinary oath in connect with an affidavit. (Op. Atty. Gen. (1917) 12 St. Dept. Rep. 507.)

SUMMARY

1. A public officer who has a duty expressly imposed by law must do so without fee or reward, unless the law allows such.

2. When a fee is allowed, a public officer may not charge more than what is allowed.

3. A person shall not request any fee unless the service has been provided by him, but may demand the fee in advanced when the law allows so.

4. A person who violated this section in liable for treble damages, as well as criminal liability.

A notary public subjects himself to criminal prosecution, civil suit, and removal by asking or receiving a higher fee then allowed for administering the ordinary oath with an affidavit.

TRUE OR FALSE?

36.   If the law allows it, a public officer may demand a fee before a duty is performed.

✓ Answer key on Page 91

Section 69 - Fee for administering certain official oaths prohibited

An officer is not entitled to a fee, for administering the oath of office to a member of the legislature, to any military officer, to an inspector of election, clerk of the poll, or to any other public officer or public employee.

SUMMARY

An officer is not entitled a fee for administering an oath of office to any public officer or public employee.

TRUE OR FALSE?

37. An officer may collect $2 for administering an oath of office to a member of the legislature.

✓ Answer key on Page 91

EXECUTIVE LAW

Misconduct by a notary and removal from office

A notary public who, in the performance of the duties of such office shall practice any fraud or deceit, is guilty of a misdemeanor (Executive Law, Section 135-a), and may be removed from office. The notary may be removed from office if the notary made a misstatement of a material fact in his application for appointment; for preparing and taking an oath of an affiant to a statement that the notary knew to be false or fraudulent.

SUMMARY

Any notary who, while using his powers practices fraud or deceit, will be guilty of a misdemeanor and may be removed from office.

TRUE OR FALSE?

38. A notary public taking an oath of an affiant to a statement that the did not know to

be false has committed a misdemeanor.

✓ Answer key on Page 91

PENAL LAW

Section 70.00 - Sentence of imprisonment for felony

2. Maximum term of sentence. The maximum term of an indeterminate sentence shall be at least three years and the term shall be fixed as follows:

    d. For a class D felony, the term shall be fixed by the court, and shall not exceed 7 years; and

    e. For a class E felony, the term shall be fixed by the court, and shall not exceed 4 years.

SUMMARY

2. The maximum term of an indefinite sentence is at least 3 years, and fixed as follows:

    d. For a class D felony, shall not exceed 7 years; and

    e. For a class E felony, shall not exceed 4 years.

TRUE OR FALSE?

39.   A felony imprisonment should not exceed 5 years.

✓ Answer key on Page 91

Section 70.15 - Sentences of imprisonment for misdemeanors and violation

1. Class A misdemeanor. A sentence of imprisonment for a class A misdemeanor shall be a definite sentence. When such a sentence is imposed the term shall be fixed by the court, and shall not exceed one year.

SUMMARY

A sentence of imprisonment for a class A misdemeanor shall be a fixed sentence, and shall not exceed 1 year.

TRUE OR FALSE?

40.   Misdemeanors imprisonments should not exceed 1 year.

✓ Answer key on Page 91

Section 170.10 - Forgery in the second degree

A person is guilty of forgery in the second degree when, with intent to defraud, deceive or injure another, he falsely makes, completes or alters a written instrument which is or purports to be, or which is calculated to become or to represent if completed:

1. A deed, will, codicil, contract, assignment, commercial instrument, or other instrument which does or may evidence, create, transfer, terminate or otherwise affect a legal right, interest, obligation or status; or

2. A public record, or an instrument filed or required or authorized by law to be filed in or with a public office or public servant; or

3. A written instrument officially issued or created by a public office, public servant or governmental instrumentality.

Forgery in the second degree is a class D felony.

SUMMARY

A person is guilty of forgery in the second degree when he intends to deceive or injure another, or if he falsely makes or alters the following written instruments:

1. A deed, will, contract, or any instrument that creates, transfers, or terminates a legal right; or

2. A public record, or an instrument to be filed in a public office or with a public servant; or

3. A written instrument created by a public office or public servant.

Forgery in the second degree is a class D felony.

TRUE OR FALSE?

41.   Forgery is a class E felony.

✓ Answer key on Page 91

Section 175.40 - Issuing a false certificate

A person is guilty of issuing a false certificate when, being a public servant authorized by law to make or issue official certificates or other official written instruments, and with intent to defraud, deceive or injure another person, he issues such an instrument, or makes the same with intent that it be issued, knowing that it contains a false statement or false information.

Issuing a false certificate is a class E felony.

SUMMARY

A public servant is guilty of issuing false certificate when he is authorized by law to make official certificates, has the intent to defraud, deceive, or injure another person, and knows that it has false statements or information.

This is a class E felony.

TRUE OR FALSE?

42.   Issuing a false certificate is a class E Felony.

✓ Answer key on Page 91

Section 195.00 - Official misconduct

A public servant is guilty of official misconduct when, with intent to obtain a benefit or to injure or deprive another person of a benefit:

   d. He commits an act relating to his office but constituting an unauthorized exercise of his official functions, knowing that such act is unauthorized; or

   e. He knowingly refrains from performing a duty which is imposed upon him by law or is clearly inherent in the nature of his office. Official misconduct is a class A misdemeanor.

SUMMARY

A public servant is guilty of misconduct when, with intent to benefit or injure:

    d. Commits and act relating to his office but is an unauthorized exercise of his powers, while knowing so.

    e. Knowingly refrains from performing his duty that is imposed by law or clearly inherent.

Official misconduct is a class A misdemeanor.

TRUE OR FALSE?

    43.   Official misconduct is a Class D felony.

✓ Answer key on Page 91

Section 182.1 - Advertising

    a. A notary public who is not an attorney licensed to practice law in the State of New York shall not falsely advertise that he or she is an attorney licensed to practice law in the State of New York or in any jurisdiction of the United States by using foreign terms including, but not limited to: abogado, mandataire, procuratore, Адвокат, 律師, and avoca.

    b. A notary public who is not an attorney licensed to practice law in the State of New York and who advertises his or her services as a notary public in a language other than English shall include in the advertisement the following disclaimer:

"I am not an attorney licensed to practice law and may not give legal advice about immigration or any other legal matter or accept fees for legal advice."

The disclaimer shall be printed clearly and conspicuously and shall be made in the same language as the advertisement. The translated disclaimer, in some but not all languages, is as follows:

    1. Simplified Chinese:
我不是有执照的律师 ，不能出庭辩护 ，不能提供有关移民事务或 其他法律事务的法律建议，也不能收取法律咨询的费用。

2. Traditional Chinese:
本人不是持牌執業律師，因此不能出庭辯護,不能向閣下提供移民 及其他法律事務方面的法律意見，也不能收取法律諮詢費

3. Spanish:
"No estoy facultado para ejercer la profesión de abogado y no puedo brindar asesoría legal sobre inmigración o ningún otro asunto legal como tampoco puedo cobrar honorarios por la asesoría legal."

4. Korean:
저는 법을 집행할 수 있는 자격이 있는 변호사가 아니며, 이민이나 또는 다른 적법한 문제나 혹은 적법한 조언에 대한 수수료를 받을 수 있는지에 대한 법률상의 조언을 드릴수 가 없을지도 모릅니다.

5. Haitian Creole:
MWEN PA AVOKA KI GEN LISANS POU PRATIKE LWA E MWEN PA KA BAY KONSÈY LEGAL SOU ZAFÈ IMIGRASYON OSWA NENPÒT KI LÒT ZAFÈ LEGAL OSWA AKSEPTE LAJEN POU BAY KONSÈY LEGAL.

SUMMARY

a. A notary public who is not an attorney shall not falsely advertise that they are an attorney by using foreign terms.

b. A notary public who advertised in a foreign language other than English shall include the following disclaimer, clearly and obviously in the same foreign language used:

"I am not an attorney licensed to practice law and may not give legal advice about immigration or any other legal matter or accept fees for legal advice."

TRUE OR FALSE?

44.   A notary public who is not an attorney needs to include a disclaimer on any advertisement that is in any language.

✓ Answer key on Page 91

MISCELLANEOUS

Member of legislature

If a member of the legislature is appointed to any civil office under for the State of New York, his acceptance shall vacate his seat in the legislature.

However, a legislature can be appointed to any office in which she will receive no salary.

Sheriffs

Sheriffs shall hold no other office.

Notary must officiate on request

A notary public must officiate on request (Penal Law Section 195) and refusing to do so is a misdemeanor.

Perjury

Perjury is knowingly giving false statements under oath or affirmation.

DEFINITIONS AND GENERAL TERMS

Acknowledgment

A formal declaration made before an officer (i.e. notary public) by a person who has executed a written instrument as his free act and deed.

A notary public should not take an acknowledgment if he has an interest in the legal instrument.

A notary public who makes a false certificate is guilty of forgery in the second degree. It is punishable by imprisonment for a term of not exceeding 7 years.

A notary public taking acknowledgments over the telephone is guilty of a misdemeanor.

Administrator

A person appointed by the court to manage the estate of a deceased person who left no will.

Affiant

The person who swears to an affidavit.

Affidavit

A sworn statement signed by the person swearing by it. It is sworn personally before a notary public or other officer who has the authority to administer an oath.

An affidavit is an ex parte statement.

Affirmation

Someone who declines to take an oath for religious, ethical, or other reasons. Instead of taking an oath, the person may affirm that certain statements are true. It is equivalent to an oath and is just as binding.

Apostile

A form of authentication issued by the Department of State. It is a notarized and county-certified document. Can be used internationally.

Attest

To be present and subscribe as a witness to the execution of a written instrument, at the request of the person who makes it.

Attestation Clause

The clause at the end of a will where the witnesses certify that the will was executed before them, and the manner of the execution of the same.

Authentication (Notarial)

A document signed by a notary public that is authenticated by a county clerk. This authenticates/verifies the authority of the notary public. Also called county clerk's certificate.

Bill of Sale

A written instrument given from a vendor (seller) to vendee (buyer) to pass title of personal property.

Certified Copy

A signed and certified public record meant to certify that it is the original copy. Only public officials that have the original copy can perform the certification. A notary public cannot issue certified copies.

Chattel

Personal property that is movable, such as household goods or fixtures. Does not include real estate.

Chattel Paper

Writing that indicates that the holder is owed money and has a security interest in valuable goods associated with the debt.

Codicil

An instrument made after a will and modifying the will in some respects.

Consideration

Anything of value (i.e. money, possessions, love, etc.) given to initiate a contract.

Contempt of Court

Disrespectful behavior towards the authority of a court which disrupts the execution of court orders.

Contract

An agreement between parties for a legal consideration.

Conveyance (Deed)

A legal document that serves as proof of a deed (or title) which creates, transfers, assigns, or surrenders any estate or interest in real property.

Deponent

A person who testifies to information or facts under oath in a deposition. A deponent is also an affiant.

Deposition

A witness's sworn out-of-court testimony under oath or by affirmation, before an authorized official. It is used at the trial or hearing.

Duress

Unlawful constraint put on a person to be forced to do some act against his will.

Escrow

An instrument that is put into the custody of a third-party to be held until the occurrence of an event.

Executor

A person named in a will to carry out the requirements of the will.

Ex Parte (From One Side Only)

A hearing or examination without requiring all of the parties to be present.

Felony

A crime punishable by death or imprisonment in a state prison.

Guardian

A person in charge of a minor's person or property.

Judgment

A decision of a court regarding the rights and liabilities of parties in a legal action or proceeding.

Jurat

The clause at the end of the document stating the date, place, and name of the officer (notary public) certifies that it was sworn to before him.

The following is generally used as a form of jurat:

"Sworn to before me this .... day of ...., 20 ......"

Laches

The delay or negligence in asserting one's legal rights.

Lease

A contract made for a consideration (i.e. rent) in which the owner of property (real estate, car, etc.) allows use of the property for a specified period of time (term).

Lien

The right to retain the possession of another person's property until the owner fulfills a legal duty to the person holding the property, such as a satisfying a debt.

Litigation

The act of carrying on a lawsuit.

Misdemeanor

Any crime other than a felony.

Mortgage On Real Property

A legal document that creates a lien on real estate as security until a debt has been satisfied.

Notary Public

A public officer who can perform many duties such as:
- Executes acknowledgments of deeds
- Administer oaths and affirmations the truthfulness of statements on documents
- Take affidavits declarations

Oath

A declaration made by the person taking it that his statements are true to his knowledge. It must be taken before an authorized person (notary public).

An oath must be administered as required by law personally in front of a notary public and cannot be administered over the telephone.

The person taking the oath must say "I do" or something similar in meaning.

A corporation or a partnership cannot take an oath.

A notary public cannot administer an oath to himself.

Plaintiff

A person or group who initiates a lawsuit against another party.

Power of Attorney

A legal document giving one person the power to act for another person.

Proof

A formal declaration made by a subscribing witness usually stating that he witnessed the signature of the signer of the document.

Protest

A formal declaration made by a notary public declaring a default in payment on a promissory note.

Seal

In NYS, notaries public are not required to use a seal. The only inscription required is the name of the notary and the words "Notary Public for the State of New York."

Signature of Notary Public

A notary public signature must use the name he was appointed. In addition to this, the following must be included:
- Venue
- Name printed, typewritten, or stamped beneath his signature in black ink
- The words "Notary Public State of New York"
- The name of the county in which he is qualified
- Date that his commission expires

Notaries public who marries during their commission may continue to use the name they were using prior to marriage. If the notary public chooses to use their married name instead, they will need to use this format as their signature and seal: name prior to marriage, followed by married name in parenthesis. When renewing their commission, they can choose to renew under their married name or the name prior to marriage.

A notary public can be appointed under a religious name if he is a member of a religious order.

Statute

A law established by an act of the Legislature.

Statute of Frauds

A state law that refers that certain kinds of contracts must be in writing so that they can be enforceable.

Statute of Limitations

A law that sets a time limit on initiating criminal prosecution or a civil action.

Subordination Clause

A clause in an agreement which states that a future mortgage takes priority over an existing mortgage.

Sunday

A notary public may administer an oath or take an affidavit or acknowledgment on Sunday, but cannot take a deposition in a civil proceeding.

Swear

To take an oath.

Taking an Acknowledgment

A notary public that is taking an acknowledgment needs to certify that the person acknowledging:

1. Tells the notary public that he is the person named in the instrument
2. Has satisfactory evidence of the identity of the person whose acknowledgment is taken.

After the requirements are met, the notary public certifies to taking the acknowledgment by signing his official signature to the form.

Venue

The location where the notarial act takes place, usually stated in the following format at the beginning of the notarial certificate or at the top of the notary's jurat or official certification:

"State of New York, County of (New York) ss.:"

Will

An instrument by which a person makes a disposition of his property to take effect after death.

SCHEDULE OF FEES

Description	Fee ($)
Appointment as Notary Public- Total Commission Fee ($40 appointment and $20 filing of Oath of Office)	60.00
Change of Name/Address	10.00
Duplicate Identification Card	10.00
Issuance of Certificate of Official Character	1.00
Filing Certificate of Official Character	1.00
Authentication Certificate	3.00
Protest of Note, Commercial Paper, etc.	0.75
Each additional Notice of Protest (limit 5) each	0.10
Oath or Affirmation	2.00
Acknowledgment (each person)	2.00
Proof of Execution (each person)	2.00
Swearing Witness	2.00

TEST-TAKING STRATEGIES

MAKE PREDICTIONS

Your mind is typically the most focused immediately after you have read the question. Try predicting the answer right before reading the answer choices. This technique is useful on questions that test objective factual knowledge. By predicting the answer before reading the available choices, you eliminate the possibility that you will be distracted or led astray by an incorrect answer choice. Scan the answers to see if your prediction is one of the choices. If it is, you can be quite confident that you have the right answer. You will feel more confident in selection if you read the question, predict the answer, and then find your prediction among the answer choices. After using this strategy, be sure to still read all of the answer choices carefully and completely.

ANSWER THE QUESTION

Test authors create some excellent answer choices that are wrong. Don't pick an answer just because it sounds right or you believe it to be true. It MUST answer the question. Don't choose an answer that is factually true but is an incorrect choice because it does not answer the question. Once you've made your selection, go back and check it against the question and make sure you didn't misread the question, and that your choice does answer the question posed. For instance, a test author might turn the question into a negative redirect the focus of the question right at the end. Avoid falling into these traps by reading the answer choices carefully.

PROCESS OF ELIMINATION

The first step in answering long and complicated questions is to make sure you understand what the question is asking. Sometimes it helps to rephrase the question into a statement, or a simpler question. Once you're sure you know what the question is asking, you'll want to begin by eliminating any answer choices that are clearly wrong. Even if doing so only eliminates one out of four or five answer choices, you've still improved your odds of choosing the correct answer choice.

DIFFICULT QUESTIONS

As much as you have prepared to take the test, it is likely that you will come across a few questions for which you simply don't know the answer. In this situation, don't waste too much time on questions that appear too hard or difficult. Follow the process of elimination stated above to try to identify any obviously incorrect answers and guess at the remaining answer choices before giving up. Carefully think about each possible choice independently from the other choices. Ask yourself if it is possible that it could be the correct answer. When going through each choice this way, you are often able to discover things you might have overlooked. After eliminating obviously wrong answers, make a selection and move on to the next question.

CONFUSING ANSWER CHOICES

There may be a tendency to focus on answer choices that are easiest to comprehend. Many people gravitate to these answer choices because they require less concentration. This is a mistake. Many people fall into this trap designed by test authors. It may be difficult to identify so read through each answer choice carefully. Give these types of questions extra attention. When you come across an answer choice that is confusing, you should give it extra attention. Try to make sense of it. If it is still confusing, set it aside and examine the remaining choices. If you are confident that another answer choice is the correct answer, you can leave the confusing answer choice aside. Otherwise, try rephrasing the confusing answer choice to make sense of it in the context of the question.

DIFFICULT WORDS

Don't choose an answer choice just because it is the only one word you recognize. If you only recognize the words in one answer choice and not the rest, make sure it is correct and really answers the question before you choose it. If you can eliminate it, then you increase your chances of getting the right answer even if you have to guess. Try dissecting difficult words. Notice prefixes and suffixes and words like *may, can, often, rarely*, etc. An answer choice may be wrong because it doesn't contain these words but has words like *exactly* and *never*, which leaves no room for exception.

SWITCHBACK WORDS

Be careful for switchback words such as *but*, *although*, and *nevertheless*. They will alter the nature of the question and are there to throw you off. Negative words, such as *not* or *except* will subtly reverse the meaning of a question. This trap can easily lead you astray if you are not paying attention to each word in the question. For example, missing the reversal word in the question "Which of the following is not...?," will cause you to answer incorrectly. You might be so confident that you will not reread the question and move on without realizing the original error. A good strategy is to underline or highlight each switchback and negative word in the question to keep track of them easily. Pay close attention to each and every word to avoid this trick.

PRACTICE TESTS

TAKING THE PRACTICE TEST

The practice tests will help you most if you take it under conditions as close as possible to those of the actual test.

- **Set aside 1 hour of uninterrupted time.**
  That way you can complete the entire test in one sitting.

- **Sit at a desk or table cleared of any other papers, books, and electronic devices.**
  You won't be able to take a dictionary, books, notes, scratch paper, phone, or laptop into the test room.

- **Record your answers on paper, then score your test.**
  Use the answer sheet when completing a practice test to simulate the real testing environment. After completing the practice test, you can score the test yourself. *Note:* The passing grade is 70%, meaning you must get at least 28 answers correct!

PRACTICE TEST 1: ANSWER SHEET

1. Ⓐ Ⓑ Ⓒ Ⓓ   11. Ⓐ Ⓑ Ⓒ Ⓓ   21. Ⓐ Ⓑ Ⓒ Ⓓ   31. Ⓐ Ⓑ Ⓒ Ⓓ

2. Ⓐ Ⓑ Ⓒ Ⓓ   12. Ⓐ Ⓑ Ⓒ Ⓓ   22. Ⓐ Ⓑ Ⓒ Ⓓ   32. Ⓐ Ⓑ Ⓒ Ⓓ

3. Ⓐ Ⓑ Ⓒ Ⓓ   13. Ⓐ Ⓑ Ⓒ Ⓓ   23. Ⓐ Ⓑ Ⓒ Ⓓ   33. Ⓐ Ⓑ Ⓒ Ⓓ

4. Ⓐ Ⓑ Ⓒ Ⓓ   14. Ⓐ Ⓑ Ⓒ Ⓓ   24. Ⓐ Ⓑ Ⓒ Ⓓ   34. Ⓐ Ⓑ Ⓒ Ⓓ

5. Ⓐ Ⓑ Ⓒ Ⓓ   15. Ⓐ Ⓑ Ⓒ Ⓓ   25. Ⓐ Ⓑ Ⓒ Ⓓ   35. Ⓐ Ⓑ Ⓒ Ⓓ

6. Ⓐ Ⓑ Ⓒ Ⓓ   16. Ⓐ Ⓑ Ⓒ Ⓓ   26. Ⓐ Ⓑ Ⓒ Ⓓ   36. Ⓐ Ⓑ Ⓒ Ⓓ

7. Ⓐ Ⓑ Ⓒ Ⓓ   17. Ⓐ Ⓑ Ⓒ Ⓓ   27. Ⓐ Ⓑ Ⓒ Ⓓ   37. Ⓐ Ⓑ Ⓒ Ⓓ

8. Ⓐ Ⓑ Ⓒ Ⓓ   18. Ⓐ Ⓑ Ⓒ Ⓓ   28. Ⓐ Ⓑ Ⓒ Ⓓ   38. Ⓐ Ⓑ Ⓒ Ⓓ

9. Ⓐ Ⓑ Ⓒ Ⓓ   19. Ⓐ Ⓑ Ⓒ Ⓓ   29. Ⓐ Ⓑ Ⓒ Ⓓ   39. Ⓐ Ⓑ Ⓒ Ⓓ

10. Ⓐ Ⓑ Ⓒ Ⓓ   20. Ⓐ Ⓑ Ⓒ Ⓓ   30. Ⓐ Ⓑ Ⓒ Ⓓ   40. Ⓐ Ⓑ Ⓒ Ⓓ

PRACTICE TEST 1

1. What is the educational requirement for a notary public?

   A. Common school education
   B. High school diploma
   C. College degree
   D. None

2. Which of the following two statements are correct? A notary public may:

   1. Solemnize a marriage
   2. Take the acknowledgment of parties and witnesses to a written contract of marriage

   A. Only 1
   B. Only 2
   C. 1 and 2
   D. None

3. When the bank of a safe deposit box opens the box in front of a notary public, the notary shall file with the lessor a certificate under seal which contains:

   1. The date of the opening of the safe deposit box
   2. The name of the lessee
   3. A list (inventory) of the contents

   A. 1 only
   B. 1 and 2 only
   C. 1, 2, and 3
   D. 3 only

4. What is the fee for a county clerk's certificate of official character?

   A. $25
   B. $50
   C. $1
   D. $5

5. Which of the following may a notary public who is duly licensed as an attorney and counselor at law in New York State substitute the words "Notary Public" for?

   A. "Attorney at Law"
   B. "Attorney and Counselor at Law"
   C. "Lawyer"
   D. "Notary Public Lawyer"

6. What is the document used as testimony in a court proceeding?

   A. Instrument
   B. Testament
   C. Deposition
   D. Subpoena

7. Which of the following convictions will bar a candidate to be appointed as a notary public?

   A. Drunken driving
   B. Misdemeanor
   C. A crime
   D. Traffic offenses

8. The following form is used in which clause?
   "Sworn to before me this _____ day

of _____"

A. Pro Se
B. The Oath
C. The Affirmation
D. Jurat

9. Which of the following is required to be a notary public?

A. Be a United States citizen
B. Be a resident of the state
C. Have a place of business in the state
D. Be a registered voter

10. What is a written instrument given to pass title of personal property from vender to vendee?

A. Affirmation
B. Bill of Sale
C. Chattel Paper
D. Codicil

11. Which of the following people can hold the office of notary public?

A. A County Sheriff
B. A former Commissioner of Deeds for NYC who was removed from office
C. A & B above
D. None of the above

12. What is the fee charged to a person for an affidavit at the county clerk's office?

A. $2
B. $2 for each original signature witnessed
C. .75 (cents) for the first one and .10 (cents) for the second one

D. Notary services are free during normal business hours

13. Any person who is not a notary public but who represents himself as such is guilty of:

A. A misdemeanor
B. A felony
C. Harassment
D. Perjury

14. Which of the following is not true when the Secretary of State issues a duplicate notary public identification card?

A. The word "duplicate" will stamped across the duplicate identification card
B. Have the same identification number as the original identification card
C. Be the exact copy as the original identification card
D. Fee of $10 will be charged for the duplicate identification card

15. At what age must a notary public be at time of application for appointment?

A. 18
B. 20
C. 21
D. 25

16. What is the maximum length of term as a notary public?

A. 6 months
B. 1 year
C. 2 years
D. 4 years

17. Which of the following acts may a notary public not do on a Sunday?

   A. Take an acknowledgment
   B. Administer an oath
   C. Take an affidavit
   D. Take a deposition

18. What is it called to witness the execution of a written instrument, at the request of the person who makes it, and subscribe the same as a witness?

   A. Endorse
   B. Attest
   C. Certifies
   D. Affirms

19. Which of the following must a person do to continue to be a notary public in NYS if he moves out of the state and does not maintain an office in NYS?

   A. Pay an additional $15 out of state fee
   B. Become a notary public in the other state
   C. Get NY driver's license
   D. None of the above

20. Which of the follow are not defects that will cause a notary public act to be deemed invalid?

   A. The action occurred on a Sunday
   B. The action was outside the jurisdiction of the notary
   C. Misspelling of his name
   D. Expiration of his term

21. What is a misdemeanor?

   A. Intentionally wrongful or improper act
   B. Any crime other than a felony
   C. Unlawful performance of an act
   D. Minor felony

22. Which of the following is not printed on a notary public identification card?

   A. Appointee's name
   B. Address and county
   C. Issued date
   D. Commission term

23. What do the witnesses to a will sign?

   A. The certificate of acknowledgment
   B. Attestation clause
   C. Identity verification form
   D. The affidavit

24. Which class felony is forgery in the second degree?

   A. B
   B. C
   C. D
   D. E

25. What is an executor?

   A. A document that verifies the authority of a notary public
   B. The placing of an instrument in the hands of a person as a depository
   C. The one named in the will to carry out the requirements of a will
   D. An instrument that modifies an already existing will

26. What is the fee for the certification of a notarial signature by a county clerk?

    A. $0.50
    B. $0.75
    C. $1
    D. $3

27. What will a notary public who knowingly makes a false certificate be prosecuted for?

    A. Forgery
    B. Misconduct
    C. A misdemeanor
    D. Malpractice

28. What does a county clerk's certificate authenticate?

    A. Authority of a notary public
    B. Authority of a county clerk
    C. Authority of the Secretary of State
    D. None of the above

29. The notary certificate of a witness to the execution of a real estate conveyance is called:

    A. Qualified resident
    B. Official Character
    C. Certificate of acknowledgment
    D. None of the above

30. Which of the following is the clause, located at the end of a will, where the witnesses certify that the instrument has been executed before them?

    A. Attestation clause
    B. Clause of will
    C. Subordination clause
    D. None of the above

31. When are conveyances of real property not be recorded?

    A. The conveyance is in a foreign language with no translations
    B. The fee of $5 is not paid before the conveyance
    C. The notary public has taken an acknowledgment from both parties prior
    D. None the above

32. What is the geographical place called where a notary public takes an affidavit or acknowledgment?

    A. State
    B. Town
    C. Locale
    D. Venue

33. Who approves the appointment of a notary public?

    A. An attorney at law from NYS
    B. County Clerk
    C. Secretary of State
    D. Town judge where the Notary resides

34. If the rental fee of a safe deposit box is not paid, the contents in the box can be removed within at least how many days?

    A. 10 days
    B. 30 days
    C. 60 days
    D. 90 days

35. Which of the following statements is not correct? A notary public is:

A. Authorized to administer oaths
B. Authorized to administer an oath to himself
C. Not authorized to administer oaths and affirmations
D. Authorized to receive and certify acknowledgments

36. What is a chattel?

A. A security agreement
B. Personal property such as household goods or fixtures
C. The Latin word for Jurat
D. The damages paid for wrongful Notary Public Fees

37. What is the following declaration a form of?

"Do you solemnly, sincerely, and truly, declare and affirm that the statements made by you are true and correct."

A. Contract
B. Conveyance
C. Affirmation
D. An oath

38. What is the rule that authorizes a deposition to be taken before a notary public in a civil proceeding?

A. Criminal Procedure Law
B. NYS Administrative Code
C. Family Court Act
D. Civil Practice Law and Rules

39. A notary public is BEST described as a(n):

A. Public official
B. Public officer
C. Legal counsel
D. Actuary

40. A statement sworn before a notary public personally signed by the affiant is an example of which of the following?

A. Codicil
B. Affidavit
C. Jurat
D. Oath

PRACTICE TEST 1: ANSWER KEY

1. A. Common school education

Section 130 – Appointment of Notaries Public .... Page 4

2. D. None

Section 11 – Domestic Relations Law .... Page 37

3. C. 1, 2, and 3

Section 335 – Banking Law .... Page 36

4. C. $1

Section 132 – Certificates of official character of notaries public .... Page 9

5. B. "Attorney and Counselor at Law"

Section 137 – Statement as to authority of notaries public .... Page 19

6. C. Deposition

Deposition .... Page 53

7. C. A crime

Section 130 – Appointment of Notaries Public .... Page 4

8. D. Jurat

Jurat .... Page 54

9. A. Be a United States citizen

Section 130 – Appointment of Notaries Public .... Page 4

10. B. Bill of Sale

Bill of Sale .... Page 52

11. D. None of the above

Member of Legislature & Sheriffs .... Page 50

Section 140 – Executive Law .... Page 11

12. D. Notary services are free during normal business hours

Section 534 – County Law .... Page 12

13. A. A misdemeanor

Public Officers Laws .... Page 42

14. C. Be the exact copy as the original I.D. card

Section 131 – Procedure of appointment; fees and commissions .... Page 6

15. A. 18

Become a Notary Public in New York .... Page ii

16. D. 4 years

Section 130 – Appointment of Notaries Public .... Page 4

34. B. 30 days

Section 335 – Banking Law .... Page 36

35. C. Not authorized to administer oaths and affirmations

Section 135 – Powers and duties .... Page 14

36. B. Personal property such as household goods or fixtures

Chattel .... Page 52

37. D. An oath

Affirmation .... Page 51

38. D. Civil Practice Law and Rules

Rule 3113 – Civil Practice Law and Rules .... Page 37

39. B. Public officer

Public Officers Laws .... Page 42

40. B. Affidavit

Affidavit .... Page 51

PRACTICE TEST 2: ANSWER SHEET

1. Ⓐ Ⓑ Ⓒ Ⓓ   11. Ⓐ Ⓑ Ⓒ Ⓓ   21. Ⓐ Ⓑ Ⓒ Ⓓ   31. Ⓐ Ⓑ Ⓒ Ⓓ

2. Ⓐ Ⓑ Ⓒ Ⓓ   12. Ⓐ Ⓑ Ⓒ Ⓓ   22. Ⓐ Ⓑ Ⓒ Ⓓ   32. Ⓐ Ⓑ Ⓒ Ⓓ

3. Ⓐ Ⓑ Ⓒ Ⓓ   13. Ⓐ Ⓑ Ⓒ Ⓓ   23. Ⓐ Ⓑ Ⓒ Ⓓ   33. Ⓐ Ⓑ Ⓒ Ⓓ

4. Ⓐ Ⓑ Ⓒ Ⓓ   14. Ⓐ Ⓑ Ⓒ Ⓓ   24. Ⓐ Ⓑ Ⓒ Ⓓ   34. Ⓐ Ⓑ Ⓒ Ⓓ

5. Ⓐ Ⓑ Ⓒ Ⓓ   15. Ⓐ Ⓑ Ⓒ Ⓓ   25. Ⓐ Ⓑ Ⓒ Ⓓ   35. Ⓐ Ⓑ Ⓒ Ⓓ

6. Ⓐ Ⓑ Ⓒ Ⓓ   16. Ⓐ Ⓑ Ⓒ Ⓓ   26. Ⓐ Ⓑ Ⓒ Ⓓ   36. Ⓐ Ⓑ Ⓒ Ⓓ

7. Ⓐ Ⓑ Ⓒ Ⓓ   17. Ⓐ Ⓑ Ⓒ Ⓓ   27. Ⓐ Ⓑ Ⓒ Ⓓ   37. Ⓐ Ⓑ Ⓒ Ⓓ

8. Ⓐ Ⓑ Ⓒ Ⓓ   18. Ⓐ Ⓑ Ⓒ Ⓓ   28. Ⓐ Ⓑ Ⓒ Ⓓ   38. Ⓐ Ⓑ Ⓒ Ⓓ

9. Ⓐ Ⓑ Ⓒ Ⓓ   19. Ⓐ Ⓑ Ⓒ Ⓓ   29. Ⓐ Ⓑ Ⓒ Ⓓ   39. Ⓐ Ⓑ Ⓒ Ⓓ

10. Ⓐ Ⓑ Ⓒ Ⓓ   20. Ⓐ Ⓑ Ⓒ Ⓓ   30. Ⓐ Ⓑ Ⓒ Ⓓ   40. Ⓐ Ⓑ Ⓒ Ⓓ

PRACTICE TEST 2

1. A person named by a court to administer the estate of a man who has died without leaving a will is called the:

   A. Executor
   B. Intestate
   C. Administrator
   D. Surrogate

2. Which of the following acts can be performed by a notary public on Sunday?

   A. Certified original certificate of government doc photocopy
   B. Affidavit
   C. Someone's signature to their own will by non-attorney notary
   D. A contract of marriage

3. Which degree in forgery is a person guilty of when he has the intent to defraud, injure or deceive another?

   A. First
   B. Second
   C. Third
   D. Fourth

4. Who has some limited rights to practice law as a non-attorney?

   A. Law students after 2 semesters and have not failed bar exam 2 times
   B. Officers for the prevention of cruelty
   C. Law school graduates
   D. All the above

5. A notary public may not be removed from office for misconduct unless the person:

   1. is served with a copy of the charges against him or her
   2. has had an opportunity to be heard

   A. 1 and 2 are not correct
   B. Only 1 is correct
   C. Only 2 is correct
   D. 1 and 2 are correct

6. What is an apostile?

   A. An authentication certified for international use
   B. A notary public application
   C. Class D felony
   D. The administrator of a will appointed by the court

7. What is it called when a notary public declares the following statement on an affidavit?

   "Sworn to before me this _____ day of _____, 20_____"

   A. Codicil
   B. Contract
   C. Jurat
   D. Lien

8. What is the total commission fee for the appointment of a notary public?

   A. $10

B. $20
C. $60
D. None of the above

9. The signature and seal of a county clerk upon a certificate of the official character of a notary public may be:

A. Printed or photographed
B. Engraved
C. A facsimile
D. All of the above

10. What is "laches"?

A. A device to lock a notary logbook safely away from the public
B. The act of carrying on a lawsuit.
C. The delay or negligence in asserting one's rights in court
D. None of the above

11. Who is a notary entitled to collect a fee from for administering the oath of office?

A. Member of the legislature
B. A military officer
C. A clerk of the poll
D. None of the above

12. What is the name of what a notary public places beneath his signature?

A. Seal
B. Stamp
C. Statement of Authority
D. Certification

13. A person who subscribes their signature on an affidavit is called:

A. The executor
B. The legatee
C. The plaintiff
D. The affiant

14. Which of the following is a notary public guilty of when he takes an acknowledgment over the telephone?

A. Forgery
B. Misdemeanor
C. Felony
D. None of the above

15. Which scenario does not disqualify a notary public from performing notary duties?

A. A notary public who is a grantee in a conveyance
B. A notary public who is a mortgagor in a conveyance
C. A notary public beneficially interested in a conveyance
D. None of the above

16. What is every instrument in writing, except a will, that transfers real estate interests?

A. Conveyance
B. Escrow
C. Vendor receipt
D. Duress

17. Which law specifies the time during which a civil action or criminal prosecution must be started?

A. The law of venue

B. The statute of limitations
C. The statute of frauds
D. None of the above

18. What is an instrument that is put into the custody of a third-party to be held until the occurrence of an event?

   A. Lien
   B. Mortgage on real property
   C. Escrow
   D. Trust

19. Which of the following is a legal right attached to a specific property until a debt is paid?

   A. Lien
   B. Mortgage on real property
   C. Laches
   D. Contract

20. Which of the following is not eligible for the office of notary public?

   A. Commissioner of elections
   B. Sheriff
   C. Member of the legislature
   D. Inspector of elections

21. What is a crime that is not a felony?

   A. Regulatory offence
   B. Misdemeanor
   C. Protest
   D. Duress

22. Which of the following acts can a notary public do if he is a shareholder and has financial interest in a corporation?

A. Protest for non-payment
B. Administer an oath to a party of the corporation
C. Take the acknowledgment of the CEO of the corporation
D. None of the above

23. What is required for an indictment for perjury on an affidavit?

   A. Affiant saying "I do" or words of like meaning after the oath is read
   B. Affiant nodding head yes
   C. Affiant putting thumb print in designated box on form
   D. All the above

24. If a notary public refuses to notarize an affidavit after all requirements are met, what is the potential maximum sentence of imprisonment?

   A. 1 month
   B. 3 months
   C. 6 months
   D. 1 year

25. Who can issue certified copies of a public record?

   A. A notary public
   B. An attorney at law
   C. A public official who holds custody of the original
   D. None of the above

26. Who can issue the certificate of official character of a notary public?

   A. The notary public named in the certificate

B. A notary public who is not named in the certificate

C. Secretary of State

D. Any public official

27. Which of the following is not an example a misdemeanor?

    A. A person found guilty of contempt of court

    B. A person removed from office performs an act as a notary public

    C. A notary public refuses to notarize an affidavit

    D. None of the above

28. Which of the following is in the requirements to become a Notary Public in New York?

    A. Be at least 18 years old

    B. No special education or common school level

    C. Be a resident of NYS

    D. All the above

29. What is the writing that indicates that the holder is owed money and has interest in specified goods?

    A. Chattel

    B. Chattel paper

    C. Certificate of acknowledgment

    D. Certificate of official character

30. What does notary public subject himself to by asking or receiving more than the statutory allowance for administering an oath in connection with an affidavit?

    1. Possible removal from office

2. Criminal prosecution
3. Civil lawsuit

    A. 3 only

    B. 1 and 3 only

    C. 1, 2, and 3

    D. 2 only

31. A sentence of imprisonment for a Class A misdemeanor will be imposed by the court and not exceed:

    A. 3 months

    B. 1 year

    C. 2 years

    D. 4 years

32. A person named in a will to administer the estate of the deceased is called the:

    A. Executor

    B. Intestate

    C. Administrator

    D. Surrogate

33. What can happen to a notary public taking acknowledgment of a conveyance who is guilty of malfeasance?

    A. May be removed from office

    B. Liable to treble damages

    C. Guilty of a misdemeanor

    D. Liable in damages to the person injured

34. Which of the following acts can a notary public do?

    A. Advertise his business

    B. Execute an acknowledgment of a will

    C. Give legal advice

D. Draw up a deed

35. What is a notary public guilty of if he makes a statement he knows to be false under oath?

    A. Malpractice
    B. Perjury
    C. Contempt of court
    D. Misdemeanor

36. Who must be with a bank employee to witness the opening of a safe deposit box that has its lease terminated?

    A. A police officer or sheriff
    B. A bank officer or employee of the lessor
    C. The lessee
    D. A notary public

37. Which of the following cases can the supreme court punish anyone for criminal contempt?

    A. Practices law unlawfully
    B. Refuses to notarize an affidavit
    C. Performs any duties of a notary

before becoming a notary public
    D. Advertises to the public that he is a notary public

38. A person who starts a civil lawsuit is called the:

    A. Appellant
    B. Defendant
    C. Plaintiff
    D. Antagonist

39. Where does the jurisdiction of a New York State notary public extend throughout?

    A. United States
    B. New York State
    C. County of residence only
    D. City of residence only

40. What is the fee to administer an oath or affirmation?

    A. 75 cents
    B. $1
    C. $2
    D. $5

PRACTICE TEST 2: ANSWER KEY

PRACTICE TEST 3: ANSWER SHEET

1. Ⓐ Ⓑ Ⓒ Ⓓ   11. Ⓐ Ⓑ Ⓒ Ⓓ   21. Ⓐ Ⓑ Ⓒ Ⓓ   31. Ⓐ Ⓑ Ⓒ Ⓓ

2. Ⓐ Ⓑ Ⓒ Ⓓ   12. Ⓐ Ⓑ Ⓒ Ⓓ   22. Ⓐ Ⓑ Ⓒ Ⓓ   32. Ⓐ Ⓑ Ⓒ Ⓓ

3. Ⓐ Ⓑ Ⓒ Ⓓ   13. Ⓐ Ⓑ Ⓒ Ⓓ   23. Ⓐ Ⓑ Ⓒ Ⓓ   33. Ⓐ Ⓑ Ⓒ Ⓓ

4. Ⓐ Ⓑ Ⓒ Ⓓ   14. Ⓐ Ⓑ Ⓒ Ⓓ   24. Ⓐ Ⓑ Ⓒ Ⓓ   34. Ⓐ Ⓑ Ⓒ Ⓓ

5. Ⓐ Ⓑ Ⓒ Ⓓ   15. Ⓐ Ⓑ Ⓒ Ⓓ   25. Ⓐ Ⓑ Ⓒ Ⓓ   35. Ⓐ Ⓑ Ⓒ Ⓓ

6. Ⓐ Ⓑ Ⓒ Ⓓ   16. Ⓐ Ⓑ Ⓒ Ⓓ   26. Ⓐ Ⓑ Ⓒ Ⓓ   36. Ⓐ Ⓑ Ⓒ Ⓓ

7. Ⓐ Ⓑ Ⓒ Ⓓ   17. Ⓐ Ⓑ Ⓒ Ⓓ   27. Ⓐ Ⓑ Ⓒ Ⓓ   37. Ⓐ Ⓑ Ⓒ Ⓓ

8. Ⓐ Ⓑ Ⓒ Ⓓ   18. Ⓐ Ⓑ Ⓒ Ⓓ   28. Ⓐ Ⓑ Ⓒ Ⓓ   38. Ⓐ Ⓑ Ⓒ Ⓓ

9. Ⓐ Ⓑ Ⓒ Ⓓ   19. Ⓐ Ⓑ Ⓒ Ⓓ   29. Ⓐ Ⓑ Ⓒ Ⓓ   39. Ⓐ Ⓑ Ⓒ Ⓓ

10. Ⓐ Ⓑ Ⓒ Ⓓ   20. Ⓐ Ⓑ Ⓒ Ⓓ   30. Ⓐ Ⓑ Ⓒ Ⓓ   40. Ⓐ Ⓑ Ⓒ Ⓓ

PRACTICE TEST 3

1. What is the maximum sentence for a class E felony?

   A. 4 years
   B. 7 years
   C. 3 years
   D. There is no limit

2. A notary public resides in Connecticut but has a business in NYS. Which of the following is he allowed to do?

   A. Administer oaths in NYS only
   B. Administer oaths in NYS and in Connecticut
   C. Give legal advice in NYS only
   D. None of the above

3. Which of the following is an ex parte statement?

   A. Deposition
   B. Acknowledgment
   C. Affidavit
   D. Conveyance

4. An acknowledgment should not be taken unless the notary public has satisfactory evidence that the person making the acknowledgment:

   A. Is the person described
   B. Has paid the $2 fee
   C. Is the person who executed the instrument
   D. A and C

5. Where can the acknowledgment of a conveyance of real property be made?

   A. Within the district the notary public is authorized to perform official duties
   B. Within the City of New York
   C. Within the county of residence the notary public is commissioned in
   D. All of the above

6. What is the fee for a duplicate notary public identification card?

   A. $5
   B. $10
   C. $15
   D. $50

7. What is it called when a person takes a solemn declaration who conscientiously decline taking an oath?

   A. Affirmation
   B. Attest
   C. Acknowledgment
   D. Affidavit

8. Which of the following fees is a notary public allowed to ask for?

   A. A fee in advance before rendering any services
   B. A fee greater than is allowed
   C. A fee for any notary public services
   D. None of the above

9. What is a formal declaration before an authorized officer by a person who has

executed an instrument that such execution is his act and deed?

A. Certified Copy
B. Chattel Paper
C. Acknowledgment
D. Conveyance

10. Which of the following is not considered forgery in the second degree?

A. Alters a public record with the intent to deceive
B. Taking an acknowledgment before taking oath of office
C. Completes a will with the intent to defraud
D. Intends to injure another by falsely making a written instrument

11. What must be stated by the subscribing witness when executing a conveyance?

A. The number of years he has owned the real property
B. His place of residence
C. The county where the conveyance is executed
D. The venue where the conveyance is executed

12. Where can a New York State notary public administer oaths and take affidavits?

A. United States
B. New York State
C. The county of residence only
D. None of the above

13. What is the county clerk fee for a

certificate of official character?

A. $1
B. $5
C. $11
D. It is a free service to the general public

14. When is it NOT illegal to take an acknowledgment over the telephone?

A. It is always illegal
B. When the notary public has satisfactory evidence that the person making it is the person described
C. When the notary public is personally acquainted with the person making it
D. When no jurat is required

15. A person appointed by the court to manage the estate of a deceased person who did not leave behind a will is called:

A. An executor
B. A plaintiff
C. An administrator
D. A deponent

16. Which of the following statement is correct when a notary public is guilty of fraudulent practice?

A. Liable in damages to the person injured
B. Liable to an action to the person injured
C. Liable for a fine up to $500
D. Liable for a fine up to $1000

17. What is the fee for taking an acknowledgment and swearing two

witnesses?

A. $4
B. $1
C. $6
D. $7.50

18. What is the state law that refers that certain contracts must be in writing so that they can be enforceable at law?

A. Contract
B. Statute of frauds
C. Statute of limitations
D. Litigation

19. Which of the follow are defects that will cause a notary public act to be deemed invalid?

A. Expiration of his term
B. Vacating of his office by change of his residence
C. The action was taken outside his jurisdiction
D. All of the above

20. What is a notary public guilty of when he issues an instrument knowing that it contains false information with the intent to defraud?

A. Issuing a false certificate
B. Official misconduct
C. Perjury
D. Duress

21. What is the minimum term of an indeterminate sentence for a class D felony?

A. 3 years
B. 4 years
C. 7 years
D. There is no minimum sentence

22. What can a person take if that person declines to take an oath because of religious reasons?

A. Codicil
B. Affirmation
C. Contract
D. Lien

23. A law enacted by the New York State legislature is called:

A. Codicil
B. Seal
C. Attestation
D. Statute

24. What is a notary public guilty of when he refuses to officiate on request?

A. Forgery
B. Perjury
C. A felony
D. A misdemeanor

25. What is it called when something that has value and is given to induce someone to enter into a contract?

A. Consideration
B. Will
C. Chattel
D. Real property

26. Which of the following instruments can a notary public who is not a lawyer

prepare?

A. A will or codicil
B. A deed or an assignment
C. A mortgage
D. None of the above

27. What must a notary public who is not a NYS attorney include if he advertises his services as a notary public in a foreign language?

A. A disclaimer written in English that states he is not an attorney
B. A disclaimer written in the same foreign language that states he is not an attorney
C. The notary public services he provides
D. None of the above

28. Which of the following is a certificate of proof or acknowledgment or oath signed by a notary public?

A. Authentication
B. Affirmation
C. Chattel Paper
D. Will

29. Which of the following statements is correct when a notary public notarizes an affidavit?

A. The notary public can negotiate a fee
B. The notary public may charge a $3 fee
C. The notary public must charge a $5 fee
D. None of the above

30. What is the formal statement by a notary public declaring a default in payment on a promissory note?

A. Affidavit
B. Jurat
C. Protest
D. Proof

31. Which of the following is the section of an affidavit where the notary public certifies that it was sworn to before him?

A. Jurat
B. Swear
C. Seal
D. Affidavit

32. What is a notary public guilty of when he knowingly refrains from performing his duty that is imposed by law?

A. Official misconduct
B. Class A misdemeanor
C. Fraudulent practice
D. A and B

33. A notary public who is an attorney at law admitted to practice in NYS may:

1. Administer an oath or affirmation
2. Take the affidavit or acknowledgment of his client in respect of any matter

A. 1 and 2 are not correct
B. Only 1 is correct
C. Only 2 is correct
D. 1 and 2 are correct

34. Under what circumstance is the notary

permitted to receive a greater fee for a service than normally allowed by law?

A. When travel expenses are incurred
B. When the affidavits exceed one printed page
C. When personal inconvenience or extenuating circumstances
D. Under no circumstance

35. What is the maximum jail sentence for a class D felony?

A. 7 years
B. 1 year
C. 3 years
D. There is no maximum sentence

36. What is the act of carrying on a lawsuit?

A. Civil suit
B. Litigation
C. Protestation
D. Perjury

37. What is a deponent?

A. One named in a will to carry out the provisions
B. The testimony of a witness taken out of court under oath/affirmation
C. The agreement which creates or provides for the security interest

D. A person who testifies to information or facts under oath in a deposition

38. Who is a notary public not allowed to administer an oath to?

A. The Secretary of State
B. A military officer
C. Himself
D. A member of the legislature

39. What do applicants for reappointment of a notary public commission submit to the county clerk?

A. Their application to the oath of office
B. A $60 non-refundable application fee
C. A "pass slip" showing that he has taken and passed the notary exam
D. A and B

40. What is the fee for a protest of non-payment or non-acceptance?

A. A. 75 cents for the first one and 10 cents for each additional notice of protest
B. $1 for the first one and 10 cents for each additional notice of protest
C. $5 for up to 4 notice of protests
D. $5 for unlimited notice of protests within 1 day

PRACTICE TEST 3: ANSWER KEY

1. **A. 4 years**
   Section 70.00 – Sentence of imprisonment for felony .... Page 45

2. **A. Administer oaths in NYS only**
   Section 130 – Appointment of Notaries Public .... Page 4

3. **C. Affidavit**
   Affidavit .... Page 51

4. **D. A and C**
   Section 303 – Requisites of acknowledgments .... Page 27

5. **D. All of the above**
   Section 298 – Acknowledgments and proofs within the state .... Page 25

6. **B. $10**
   Section 131 – Procedure of appointment; fees and commissions .... Page 6

7. **A. Affirmation**
   Affirmation .... Page 51

8. **A. A fee in advance before rendering any services**
   Section 67 – Fees of public officers .... Page 42

9. **C. Acknowledgment**
   Acknowledgment .... Page 51

10. **B. Taking an acknowledgment before taking oath of office**
    Section 170.10 – Forgery in the second degree .... Page 46

11. **B. His place of residence**
    Section 304 – Proof by subscribing witness .... Page 28

12. **B. New York State**
    Section 130 – Appointment of Notaries Public .... Page 4

13. **A. $1**
    Section 132 – Certificates of official character of notaries public .... Page 9

14. **A. It is always illegal**
    Acknowledgment .... Page 51

15. **C. An administrator**
    Administrator .... Page 51

16. **A. Liable in damages to the person injured**
    Section 330 – Officers guilty of malfeasance liable for damages .... Page 34

17. **C. $6**

TRUE OR FALSE: ANSWER KEY

1. FALSE

   A notary public vacates their position once they move out of the state and holds no place of business within NYS

2. FALSE

   A $10 fee will be requested for a duplicate card

3. TRUE

   This is permitted for a fee of $1

4. TRUE

   For a fee of $3, a county clerk will verify the certificate

5. FALSE

   Once removed, notaries public are no longer eligible to be a notary public

6. TRUE

   An inspector of elections is eligible to become a notary public

7. TRUE

   Violation of the selective service draft act or its amendments bars eligibility for the office of notary public

8. FALSE

   Staff members of a county clerk appointed to become notaries public are exempt from examination and application fees

9. FALSE

   The seal of a county clerk on an official character certificate of a notary public can be facsimile, printed, stamped, photographed, or engraved

10. TRUE

    Section 135 grants the power for notaries public to take affidavits and depositions in NYS

11. FALSE

    A notary public committing fraud is considered a misdemeanor, not a felony

12. FALSE

    A notary public who is also an attorney may advertise their legal services in foreign languages

13. TRUE

    $2 is the amount authorized to charge for an oath or affirmation and an additional $2 for each additional person

14. FALSE

An attorney may write "Attorney and Counselor at Law" under his signature

15. TRUE

It is permitted that a notary public who is a stockholder of a company may take proof to a written instrument executed to that company

16. FALSE

A person cannot file a claim for defect if the defect was known about upon when it occurred. This is prevented by subdivision 3 of section 142-a

17. FALSE

Leases for less than 3 years are not conveyances

18. TRUE

A notary public is permitted to certify a conveyance at any place within the state

19. TRUE

Married women and unmarried women have the same rights in conveyances

20. FALSE

A notary public must know or have evidence that the person taking the acknowledgment is the person it describes

21. TRUE

A subscribing witness is required to certify that he knows the person signing the conveyance

22. FALSE

A notary public also must include the addresses of any subscribing witnesses

23. FALSE

Information required under section 300 is still needed

24. FALSE

The inclusion of the location within a proof of acknowledgment is viewed as a non-substantial variance

25. TRUE

A notary public is liable for damages to an injured party for fraud or malfeasance

26. FALSE

Conveyances must be in English, or have an authenticated translation

27. FALSE

The letter must be sent within 10 days

28. TRUE

It is within the power of a notary public to take depositions in a civil proceeding

29. FALSE

It is not within the power of a notary public to take the acknowledgment for witnesses of a marriage

30. TRUE

It is within the power of a notary public to administer the oath of a public officer

31. FALSE

A law student can work under the supervision of an appellate court approved legal aid organization after 2 semesters

32. FALSE

Violation of section 484 is a misdemeanor

33. TRUE

The supreme court has the power to punish individuals for unlawful practice of law

34. TRUE

It is legal to draft legal documents if the notary public is not a lawyer, as long as he has not made it a business to practice law and offer his services as an attorney at law

35. TRUE

A notary public is allowed to perform any duties of a notary public same day his oath of office has been taken and filed

36. TRUE

If the law allows it, a public offer can demand a fee before a duty is performed as stated by subdivision 3 of section 67

37. FALSE

No fee can be collected from any public employee, including a member of the legislature, for performing an oath of office

38. FALSE

A notary public that has knowingly made a false statement is guilty of a misdemeanor

39. FALSE

Class D felony can extend to 7 years

40. TRUE

1 year is the limit for misdemeanor violations

41. FALSE

Forgery is a class D felony

42. TRUE

Issuing a false certificate is a class E felony

43. FALSE

Official misconduct is a class A misdemeanor

44. FALSE

Only when advertising in a foreign language other than English is it required to include a disclaimer on the advertisement